MANCHES

THE COMPLI

Born in 1958, Michael Crick has been following Manchester United since he was twelve, at home and away, through good times and bad. Between the ages of thirteen and sixteen he saw a run of 117 consecutive matches; this coincided with the two worst seasons in United's post-war history, ending in relegation to division two. In 1989 he and the former supporters' club chairman, David Smith, published their controversial book *Manchester United: The Betrayal of a Legend*. Crick belongs to the United Review Collectors' Club and the Association of Football Statisticians. In 1998 he was a founder and organiser of the successful Shareholders United Against Murdoch campaign.

Educated at Manchester Grammar School and New College, Oxford, Crick works as a television reporter and writer. His other books include *Militant* (1984), *Scargill and the Miners* (1985), *Jeffrey Archer: Stranger Than Fiction* (1995) and *Michael Heseltine: A Biography* (1997). He is currently writing a biography of Rupert Murdoch.

Michael Crick lives in London and Oxfordshire, but his wife and daughter claim he spends most of his time at Old Trafford.

MANCHESTER UNITED
THE COMPLETE
FACT BOOK

MICHAEL CRICK

PROFILE BOOKS

Published in Great Britain in 1999 by
Profile Books Ltd
58A Hatton Garden
London EC1N 8LX

First published by Signet in 1996 as
The Complete Manchester United Trivia Fact Book

Typeset in Oranda by MacGuru
macguru@pavilion.co.uk
Printed and bound by
St Edmundsbury Press, Bury St Edmunds

A CIP catalogue record for this book is available from
the British Library.

ISBN 1 86197 206 7

CONTENTS

INTRODUCTION

Which two players have won FA Cup winners' medals with United without ever playing for United in the FA Cup? In which game did United field sixteen full internationals? Who is the only substitute to have scored four goals in a League match? Which Munich victim never scored for England, but twice missed penalties for his country? Who scored on his United debut in four different competitions, but managed only eleven goals for the club in all? Which is the only remaining League team to have beaten United more often than United have beaten them? Which four United men have been knighted? Which two United managers played together as half-backs for Preston North End? Who has had the briefest first-team career with United? And the longest? Who was the oldest player, and the shortest and the tallest?

For the answers read on. This book is a celebration. It was first published in 1996 when United had just accomplished what no English club had ever done before – a second League and cup Double. Three years later United's achievements in the mid 1990s look rather paltry. In 1999 we not only won our third Double in six years, but a Treble with the European Cup as well. My text has required considerable revision in the last three years. What a pleasurable task it's been.

During the 1990s, Manchester United resumed their traditional place at the pinnacle of English football. Throughout the '70s and '80s, Reds' followers had always had to put up with second or even third best: first to Leeds United, Arsenal and Derby County; then occasionally to Nottingham Forest, Aston Villa or Everton; and worst of all, and almost throughout, to Liverpool. For twenty years Old Trafford regulars endured torture upon torture as the Merseyside team smashed record after record. Now we've begun to take some of those records back.

Through all those dismal years of frustrating mediocrity United fans never deserted. Some of the most revealing records in this book relate to crowd figures: United gates continued to exceed those of every other club even during times when the Old Trafford trophy cabinet was gathering nothing more than layer upon layer of fresh dust.

Manchester United are back on top – the undisputed team of the 1990s. With twelve trophies in ten seasons, Sir Alex Ferguson's side has got into the habit of feeding the loyal barmy army with the glory it craves. From Bryan Robson and Eric Cantona, through Gary Pallister and Peter Schmeichel, down to Ryan Giggs and David Beckham, Roy Keane and Dwight Yorke, Manchester United again have a world-wide reputation for thrilling packed grounds and armchair audiences with their swashbuckling flair and never-say-die tenacity.

If Bill Clinton is known as the Comeback Kid then United are undoubtedly the comeback kids. The world sat in disbelief as famously we came back against Bayern Munich in the 1999 European Cup final; we did it when Peter Schmeichel saved Dennis Bergkamp's last minute penalty at Villa Park in the Cup semi-final; and we did it after being 2–0 down in Turin. But glance through the records and you'll see how often it's happened before. In seven successive FA Cup semi-finals, for example, the team has recovered from being a goal down. Any United fan who leaves a game before the very last micro-second of injury time is taking a huge risk.

This is more than just an 'Old Trafford Book of Records'. It delves into many of the quirks and twists of club history, the strange coincidences and bizarre tales of well over a century of United football. In some cases, it puts the record straight. Duncan Edwards, for example, was not the youngest man to play for United; nor did Bryan Robson score the quickest-ever goal in a World Cup finals match. But while old favourites may occasionally have to be ditched, there are plenty more records to take their place, achievements of which even the most devoted fan may not be aware, titbits and trivia to amuse and intrigue for hours.

In assembling these United records and statistics 1 have applied certain basic rules. Unlike cricket, there is no real definition of a first-class match, so I have set my own standard. As well as the three top domestic competitions and the three major European tournaments I also include three long-established 'decider' contests – the Charity Shield, the World Club Championship and the European Super Cup. And that is all. I have counted none of the numerous, short-lived Mickey Mouse contests United have occasionally been persuaded to take part in, such as the Watney Cup, the Anglo-Italian Tournament, the Screen Sport Super Cup and the Football League Centenary Trophy. Nor do I pay any attention to the temporary handles of various commercial sponsors. To me it will always be the League, the League Cup and the FA Cup. Indeed, it would be foolish to talk of anything else now that Littlewoods have pulled off the highly confusing trick of sponsoring first the League Cup and now the FA Cup.

Some record-keepers – notably the editors of those soccer bibles, the *Rothmans* books – have assembled separate statistics for the new Premier League which began in 1992. This, I feel, is a pretty futile activity, and rather insulting to the 104 years of League football that went before. Who really cares whether some player's performance is the best since August 1992? How the present stars match up to a hundred years of history is what counts. The Premiership is the product of excessive greed and media hype, but in practice it means little more than a change of name. All the essential characteristics of the good old-fashioned first division remain – the same teams (more or less), the same structure and the same basic rules. I will never forgive the founders of the Premiership for the trouble and confusion the new set-up has caused us football statisticians.

This *Fact Book* has been compiled during hundreds of hours of misspent time over the past twelve years, as I allowed myself to be distracted from more urgent tasks. I hate to think how much time I must have frittered away as I sat combing through reference books, old United programmes and magazines, and the 300-plus books that have now been published about the club and its players. I would have been lost, however, without Ian Morrison and Alan Shury's *Manchester United: A Complete Record* (Breedon, 1992), and I also used several other volumes in Breedon's wonderful *Complete Record* series. Garth Dykes's *The United Alphabet* (ACL & Polar, 1994) is one of the best statistical books ever written about United, and has that rare combination of being both astonishingly accurate and beautifully produced. Other useful publications included *Manchester United: Pictorial History and Club Record* by Charles Zahra, Iain McCartney and others (Temple Nostalgia Press, 1986), Steve Cawley and Gary James's magnificent *The Pride of Manchester* (ACL & Polar, 1991), the annual *Manchester United Handbooks*, and Phil Bradley's *Manchester United Annual* (Words on Sport, 1995). Particularly revealing, and a most enjoyable read if you can find it, is Alf Clarke's highly anecdotal 1951 history, *Manchester United* (Convoy).

Of the more general literature, I must have consulted all

twenty-nine volumes of the *Rothmans Football Yearbook* (Headline). Brian Tabner's *Through The Turnstiles* (Yore Publications, 1992) was a great help with crowd statistics. I am indebted also to the regular reports from the Association of Football Statisticians, which inspired and supplied much of the material. Unless specified otherwise, all details are to 1 August 1999.

Three United statisticians, Iain McCartney, Steve Cawley and Mike Cox, took the trouble to read drafts of my manuscript and made numerous helpful suggestions. Cox supplied the material on penalty misses. I was also assisted by Tony Brown, Mike Dobbin and Paul Wheeldon. All remaining errors are entirely mine, of course. If you spot any I'll be somewhat annoyed, but please do let me know (write to me care of the publisher) so that at least they can be corrected in future.

Michael Crick
August 1999

ABBREVIATIONS

(a)	away game
agg.	aggregate score over two legs
CS	Charity Shield
d1	division one
d2	division two
d3	division three
ECC	European Champions' Cup, better known as the European Cup, and now the European Champions' League
ECL	European Champions' League
ECWC	European Cup-Winners' Cup
FA	Football Association
FAC	FA Cup
(h)	home game
ICFC	Inter Cities Fairs Cup
LC	League Cup
(n)	game on neutral ground
OT	Old Trafford
(pr)	Premier League
SF	semi-final
so	sent off
UEFA	Union of European Football Associations (also denotes the UEFA Cup)
(W)	Wembley

1 HONOURS AND TITLES

THE TREBLE

⚽ In 1999 Manchester United became the first team in English football history to win the Treble – the League, the FA Cup and the European Cup – in the same season. Several teams had previously come close to winning the Treble:

> ⚽ In 1957 United won the League, but lost to Aston Villa in the FA Cup final and to Real Madrid in the European Cup semi-final;
> ⚽ In 1970 Leeds United came second to Everton in the League, lost to Chelsea in the FA Cup final and lost to Celtic in the European Cup semi-final;
> ⚽ In 1977 Liverpool won both the League and the European Cup, but lost to United in the FA Cup final.

⚽ In addition, Liverpool won an inferior Treble of League, League Cup and European Cup in 1984.

⚽ Three other sides in the history of European football have won Trebles of their domestic league and cup competitions together with the European Cup – Celtic in 1967, Ajax in 1972 and PSV Eindhoven in 1988. In the 1971–72 season Ajax also won the European Super Cup and the World Club Championship.

THE DOUBLE

⚽ In winning both the League and the FA Cup in 1999

United achieved the Double for the third time in just six seasons. Only five other clubs have ever won the Double, on six occasions in all – Preston North End (1889), Aston Villa (1897), Tottenham Hotspur (1961), Arsenal (1971 and 1998) and Liverpool (1986). United have won three of the nine Doubles in English history, and three of the seven won this century.

◉ In 1995 United came within three goals of winning a further double, and came the closest that any side has been to retaining both trophies. One more goal in the final league match at West Ham and two goals in the FA Cup final against Everton would have paved the way for four Doubles in six seasons.

LEAGUE TITLES

◉ United have won the League twelve times – in 1908, 1911, 1952, 1956, 1957, 1965, 1967, 1993, 1994, 1996, 1997 and 1999. This compares with Liverpool's eighteen championship titles and Arsenal's eleven.

◉ United's five League titles in seven seasons between 1993 and 1999 have been matched only by Aston Villa (5 titles between 1894 and 1900) and Liverpool (10 titles between 1976 and 1990).

◉ The following table compares each United title team using the old two-points-for-a-win system, and compensates for differences in the number of games played each season by ranking according to the percentage of possible points gained. It uses goal difference rather than the old goal average.

	Season	P	W	D	L	F	A	Pts	%
1.	1993–94	42	27	11	4	80	38	65	77.38
2.	1956–57	42	28	8	6	103	54	64	76.19
3.	1998–99	38	22	13	3	80	37	57	75.00
4.	1995–96	38	25	7	6	73	35	57	75.00
5.	1964–65	42	26	9	7	89	39	61	72.62
6.	1966–67	42	24	12	6	84	45	60	71.43
7.	1992–93	42	24	12	6	67	31	60	71.43
8.	1955–56	42	25	10	7	83	51	60	71.43
9.	1996–97	38	21	12	5	76	44	54	71.05
10.	1907–08	38	23	6	9	81	48	52	68.42
11.	1910–11	38	22	8	8	72	40	52	68.42
12.	1951–52	42	23	11	8	95	52	57	67.86

⚽ Under the old two-points-for-a-win system the 1993–94 side emerges by a margin of one point as the most successful United league side of all time. Yet using the modern three-points-for-a-win both the 1993–94 team and the 1955–56 side would gain 92 points and the Busby team would stand on top with the better goal difference. Take your pick!

⚽ United won the League by 11 points over Blackpool in 1956, which effectively remains the best winning margin of all time. It translates into 16 points under the present three-points-for-a-win system, and thus surpasses Everton's 13-point margin in 1985.

⚽ After winning the League in 1967, United had to wait twenty-six years before winning it again in 1993. But in four separate campaigns during the intervening period – 1967–68, 1971–72, 1985–86 and 1991–92 – United had been hot favourites to take the title, but then stumbled. In ten of the 'wilderness years' United had been top of the table at some point: the four seasons above, plus 1975–76, 1979–80,

1981–82, 1982–83, 1983–84 and 1987–88.

⚽ United won the League title in 1992–93, having been bottom of the table after the first two matches of the season. (This caused the Daily Mirror to run the backpage headline 'FERGIE'S BOTTOM!' – in the issue that carried photos showing Sarah Ferguson topless.)

⚽ The 92 points in 1993–94 is a record for the top division under three-points-for-a-win. Under the old two points-for-a-win regime, five teams secured more than its equivalent of 65 points, most notably Liverpool in 1978–79 with 68.

⚽ United, League runners-up in 1994–95, would have been champions under the old points system. Instead of Blackburn Rovers winning by 89 points to United's 88, both clubs would have finished with 62 points but United would have taken the title on goal difference (or goal average if that had still been in use). This is the only time the switch to three-points-for-a-win has changed the destiny of the title.

⚽ United's total of 52 points in winning the League in 1908 was then a record.

⚽ The inter-war Italian manager, Vittorio Pozzo, is said to have modelled his 1930s World Cup-winning sides on United's 1908 championship team. Pozzo had been a student in Manchester at the time.

⚽ In 1993 it took a Frenchman, Eric Cantona, to become the first player to win English league championship medals in successive seasons with different clubs. In all, Cantona won championship medals in four consecutive seasons and then six seasons out of seven: in 1991 with Marseille, in 1992 with Leeds United, and in 1993, 1994, 1996 and 1997 with United.

⚽ John Aston Senior (1952) and Junior (1967) are the only known father and son to win League championship medals with the same club.

⚽ United are one of ten clubs who have never played below the top two divisions since their entry to the League. The other nine are: Arsenal, Chelsea, Everton, Leeds United, Leicester City, Liverpool, Newcastle United, Tottenham Hotspur and West Ham United.

TROPHY TOTALS

⚽ United have now won twenty-six major trophies: twelve League titles, ten FA Cups, one League Cup, two European Cups and one European Cup-Winners' Cup. Liverpool have won thirty-four major trophies, Arsenal twenty-two and Aston Villa twenty.

⚽ In 1994 United also became the first club to win the League, FA Cup and Charity Shield in the same season.

⚽ United have won trophies in five consecutive seasons – 1989–90, 1990–91, 1991–92, 1992–93 and 1993–94 – only the second club to have accomplished this feat. Between 1976 and 1984 Liverpool won honours in nine successive seasons.

⚽ In also reaching the League Cup final in 1994, where they lost 3–1 to Aston Villa, United came the closest-ever to the Treble of all three domestic trophies. They were also the only club ever to come either first or second in each of the three main domestic competitions in the same year.

⚽ United, along with Liverpool, Tottenham Hotspur and Arsenal, are the only clubs to have won five of the six major trophies contested by English clubs – the League, FA Cup, League Cup, European Cup, European Cup Winners' Cup and UEFA Cup.

⚽ Manchester United and Manchester City have occasionally won honours together. In 1956 United won the League and City the FA Cup, and in 1968 United won the European Cup and City won the League.

⚽ When United won the second-division title in 1975, Aston Villa came second and Norwich City were third. Exactly the same positions were achieved when United won the League in 1993.

CHARITY SHIELD

⚽ Since winning the very first FA Charity Shield against the Southern League champions, Queen's Park Rangers, in 1908, United have won the trophy a record ten times. On four other occasions United shared the trophy after the match ended in a draw (sharing it three times with Liverpool – in 1965, 1977 and 1990). After beating United in both 1998 and 1999 Arsenal have now won the Shield nine times.

⚽ United's 8–4 win over Swindon Town in the 1911 Charity Shield remains the highest score and the highest aggregate score in the history of the competition. It is also the highest aggregate score in any competitive match in which United have played.

PLAYER MEDALS

⚽ Denis Irwin, Peter Schmeichel and Ryan Giggs have all won ten medals as a United player. Giggs and Schmeichel won exactly the same trophies – five League titles (1993, 1994, 1996, 1997 and 1999), three FA Cups (1994, 1996 and 1999), one League Cup (1992) and the European Cup (1999). Irwin missed the 1999 FA Cup final through suspension, but did win a European Cup-Winners' Cup medal in 1991.

⚽ Three United players – Peter Schmeichel, Ryan Giggs and Roy Keane – have three sets of Double medals, from 1994, 1996 and 1999.

⚽ Nine other United players have two sets of Double medals – Denis Irwin, Gary Pallister, Lee Sharpe and Eric

Cantona (1994 and 1996), and Gary Neville, Phil Neville, David Beckham, Paul Scholes and Andy Cole (1996 and 1999). Denis Irwin missed a third set of Double medals in 1999 through being suspended for the FA Cup final even though he had played in six of United's seven other FA Cup matches.

⚽ Ninety eight players in English history have won the Double – twenty six with United – but no player outside United has even managed to win the Double more than once.

⚽ Eric Cantona won five League titles and two FA Cup medals in just 218 games for Leeds United and Manchester United between 1992 and 1997. This is almost certainly the most concentrated record of success by any player in English history. He also won four Charity Shield medals and scored 96 goals (14 for Leeds and 82 for United).

PLAYER AWARDS

⚽ Only four United players have won the Football Writers' Association Footballer of the Year award since its inception in 1948:

1949	Johnny Carey
1966	Bobby Charlton
1968	George Best
1996	Eric Cantona

⚽ George Best is the youngest-ever Footballer of the Year. He was only 21 when awarded the title in 1968.

⚽ United players have won the Professional Footballers' Association (PFA) Player of the Year award on four occasions since it started in 1974:

1989	Mark Hughes
1991	Mark Hughes
1992	Gary Pallister
1994	Eric Cantona

⚽ Mark Hughes was the first player to win the PFA award twice, in 1989 and 1991, a feat since emulated by Alan Shearer.

⚽ From 1989 to 1994 United dominated the PFA awards. In the two years when the main award did not go to a United star, it went to former United players – David Platt in 1990, and Paul McGrath in 1993.

⚽ United players have won the PFA Young Player of the Year award on five occasions:

1985	Mark Hughes
1991	Lee Sharpe
1992	Ryan Giggs
1993	Ryan Giggs
1997	David Beckham

⚽ United players won the PFA Young Player award three years running between 1991 and 1993. In addition, Andy Cole won the Young Player title the following year, 1994, while he was still with Newcastle United.

⚽ Ryan Giggs was the first player to win the PFA Young Player award twice, in 1992 and 1993, though this was later matched by Robbie Fowler.

⚽ United are the only club to have won doubles in the main PFA awards in two consecutive seasons. The PFA Player and Young Player trophies were presented to Mark Hughes and Lee Sharpe in 1991, and to Gary Pallister and Ryan Giggs in 1992.

⚽ Mark Hughes is the only player to have received three

PFA awards. His two Player of the Year titles in 1989 and 1991 were preceded by the Young Player award in 1985.

◉ In 1994 Eric Cantona became the first foreign player to be voted PFA Player of the Year.

◉ In the spring of 1995 United could boast six players who had won ten PFA awards between them – Mark Hughes, Gary Pallister, Eric Cantona, Lee Sharpe, Ryan Giggs and Andy Cole – though the six never played together in the same side. In addition, David Beckham was to win the Young Player award two years later.

◉ Three former Scottish Footballers of the Year later signed for United – Martin Buchan (1971), Gordon Strachan (1980) and Brian McClair (1987).

KNIGHTHOODS

◉ In 1999 Alex Ferguson became the fourth man associated with United to receive a knighthood:

1968	Sir Matt Busby	Manager, 1945–71
1978	Sir Walter Winterbottom	Player, 1936–37 (later England manager)
1994	Sir Bobby Charlton	Player, 1956–73
1999	Sir Alex Ferguson	Manager, 1986 to date

2 UNITED EUROPE

EUROPEAN CUP

⚽ United's 1999 European Cup final win over Bayern Munich was the first time the direction of the final has been overturned in injury time. When the clock reached 90 minutes, United were losing 1–0 but then snatched the cup away from Bayern with quick goals from Teddy Sheringham and Ole Gunnar Solskjaer.

⚽ United have now won the European Cup twice – in 1968 and 1999 – and join a group of ten clubs to have won the trophy more than once. The others are: Real Madrid, Benfica, Inter Milan, AC Milan, Ajax, Bayern Munich, Liverpool, Nottingham Forest and Juventus.

⚽ United have now played eighty-two matches in the European Cup, more than any other English club. Liverpool have played seventy-seven matches in the competition. United's record is exceeded by thirteen other European sides – Real Madrid (197), Benfica (149), Bayern Munich (125), Juventus (120), Ajax (113), AC Milan (108), Dynamo Kiev (102), Anderlecht (98), Rangers (91), CSKA Sofia (90), Red Star Belgrade (86), Barcelona (84), Porto (84) and equalled by Celtic (82). Leeds United have played 22 games in the European Cup, Nottingham Forest 20 and Arsenal 16.

⚽ English teams have now won the European Cup nine times, compared with Italy's ten times. Spain has won the European Cup eight times, the Netherlands six and Germany five. England's wins have been shared by four different clubs – United (2), Liverpool (4), Nottingham Forest (2) and Aston Villa (1), compared with only three clubs from each of Italy, Germany and the Netherlands. English teams have lost in the European Cup final only twice in eleven appearances.

⚽ Since losing 1–0 at Juventus in December 1997, United have gone fifteen European Cup matches without defeat, though this run includes the 1998 quarter-final knock-out by Monaco on the away goals rule.

⚽ In his last game for the club against Bayern Munich in the 1999 European Cup final, Peter Schmeichel not only captained the team to a sensational victory but he also took the record for the most appearances by a United player in the competition. The leading European Cup appearances are:

Peter Schmeichel	1993–99	36 apps
Bill Foulkes	1956–69	35 apps
Denis Irwin	1993–99	34 apps
Gary Neville	1993–99	33 apps
David Beckham	1994–99	31 apps
Nicky Butt	1994–99	30 apps
Bobby Charlton	1957–69	28 apps

⚽ Denis Law stills holds the record for the most goals by any United player in the European Cup. The top scorers are:

Denis Law	1965–69	14 goals
Dennis Viollet	1956–58	13 goals
Tommy Taylor	1956–58	11 goals
Andy Cole	1996–99	11 goals
Bobby Charlton	1957–69	10 goals
Ryan Giggs	1993–99	10 goals
George Best	1965–69	9 goals
Dwight Yorke	1998–99	8 goals

◉ United reached the semi-finals in their first five attempts at the European Cup.

◉ In 1968 United became the first English side to win the European Cup. Brian Kidd scored a goal in the final on his nineteenth birthday.

◉ When United drew 3–3 with Galatasaray in October 1993, it ended a sequence of seventeen successive home wins in the European Cup stretching back to September 1957.

◉ United were the only British club to win both the European Cup (1968 and 1999) and the old European Cup-Winners' Cup (1991). Seven continental sides also achieved this – Barcelona, Bayern Munich, AC Milan, SV Hamburg, Juventus, Ajax Amsterdam and Borussia Dortmund. Juventus, Barcelona, Ajax and Bayern have all gone one further than United by winning the UEFA Cup as well.

◉ AC Milan, Juventus, Ajax and Barcelona all share United's achievement in having won both the two old senior competitions and also the European Super Cup (which United won in 1991).

◉ When the Turkish club Fenerbahçe won 1-0 at Old Trafford in October 1996 it ended United's record of 57 home games unbeaten in Europe in more than forty years. The Reds then lost two of the next three European home games as well.

THE MUNICH AIR DISASTER

◉ On 6 February 1958, United suffered the worst disaster ever to befall a British football team. While returning from a European Cup match against Red Star Belgrade, United's plane crashed during take-off from Munich Airport. Seven players were killed: Geoff Bent, Roger Byrne, Eddie Colman, Mark Jones, David Pegg, Tommy Taylor and Billy Whelan;

Duncan Edwards died from his injuries in hospital three weeks later. Three club officials – secretary Walter Crickmer, trainer Tom Curry and team coach Bert Whalley – were also killed, along with eight journalists (including former Manchester City and England goalkeeper Frank Swift), two other passengers and two members of the aircrew. Two other players – Jackie Blanchflower and Johnny Berry – suffered such serious injuries that they never played first-class football again.

⚽ In 1958, as a mark of sympathy after the Munich air disaster, UEFA invited United to participate in the 1958–59 European Cup, but a joint League-FA inquiry stopped the club from doing so, on the grounds that they were not League champions. United had already been drawn against Young Boys Berne, and so played the fixtures as friendlies instead and won 3–2 on aggregate. Young Boys went on to reach the European Cup semi-final.

EUROPEAN FIXTURES

⚽ United have qualified 23 times for European competition (including the 1999–2000 Season) – more than any other English club with the exception of Liverpool, who have qualified 26 times. Arsenal have qualified for Europe fifteen times, followed by both Leeds United and Cardiff City with fourteen entries.

⚽ Without the 1985–90 ban on English clubs from Europe, United would have qualified for the European Cup-Winners' Cup in 1985, and for the UEFA Cup in 1988 (and possibly also in 1986).

⚽ United have played European away fixtures in 26 different countries (in order of first visit): Belgium, West Germany, Spain, Ireland, Czechoslovakia, Yugoslavia, Italy, Netherlands, England, Portugal, Sweden, France, Hungary, Finland,

East Germany, Malta, Poland, Austria, Bulgaria, Scotland, Wales, Greece, Russia, Turkey, Slovakia and Denmark.

⚽ United's most frequent opponents in European competition have been Juventus, whom the Reds have played ten times in five different seasons and in all three competitions:

1976–77	UEFA	1–0 (h); 0–3 (a); agg: 1–3
1983–84	ECWC s-f	1–1 (h); 1–2 (a); agg: 2–3
1996–97	ECC	0–1 (a); 0–1 (h)
1997–98	ECC	3–2 (h); 0–1 (a)
1998–99	ECC s-f	1–1 (h); 3–2 (a); agg: 4–3

⚽ United have been paired against Barcelona four times – in 1983–84, 1990–91, 1994–95 and 1998–99.

⚽ United have met five different Spanish clubs in Europe – Athletic Bilbao, Real Madrid, Valencia, Barcelona, and Atlético Madrid – and five Hungarian sides – Ferencváros, Raba Vasas ETO, Videoton, Pecsi Munkas and Kispest Honved.

EUROPEAN RESULTS

⚽ United's best home scores in Europe have been:

ECC	10–0	v. Anderlecht	19 September 1956
ECWC	6–1	v. Willem II	15 October 1963
ICFC/UEFA	6–1	v. Djurgårdens	27 October 1964

⚽ The three above games were each the first home match that United played in each competition.

⚽ United's best away scores in Europe have been:

ECC	6–0	v. Shamrock Rovers	25 September 1957
ECWC	3–1	v. Legia Warsaw	10 April 1991

ICFC/UEFA	6–1	v. Borussia Dortmund	11 November 1964
	5–0	v. Strasbourg	12 May 1965

⚽ United's best aggregate victories in Europe have been:

ECC	12–0	v. Anderlecht	1956–57
ECWC	7–2	v. Willem II	1963–64
ICFC/UEFA	10–1	v. Borussia Dortmund	1964–65

⚽ United's best scores in the group sections of the new European Champions League have been:

home:	5–0	v. Brondby	4 November 1998
away:	6–2	v. Brondby	21 October 1998

⚽ United's only three home defeats in Europe were all by 1–0, and all in the same season:

ECL	0–1	v. Fenerbahçe	30 October 1996
	0–1	v. Juventus	20 November 1996
	0–1	v. Borussia Dortmund	23 April 1997

⚽ United's worst away defeats in Europe have been:

ECC/ECL	0–4	v. AC Milan	14 May 1958
	0–4	v. Barcelona	2 November 1994
ECWC	0–5	v. Sporting Lisbon	18 March 1964
ICFC/UEFA	0–3	v. Juventus	3 November 1976

⚽ United's worst aggregate defeats in Europe have been:

ECC	2–5	v. AC Milan	1957–58
ECWC	1–4	v. Atlético Madrid	1991–92

⚽ In eight visits to Spanish clubs United have never managed to win, having lost six times and drawn just twice. United's only victory in Spain came in the 1999 European Cup final against Bayern Munich.

⚽ Only once in 52 European two-legged ties have United won on the away-goals rule – against Dukla Prague in 1983. They have lost on away goals four times – to Widzew Lodz in 1981, Galatasaray in 1993, Rotor Volgograd in 1995 and Monaco in 1998.

⚽ United have lost on penalties on the only two occasions on which this method was used to decide one of their European ties – against Videoton in 1985 and Torpedo Moscow in 1992, both in the UEFA Cup.

EUROPEAN CUP-WINNERS' CUP

⚽ Alex Ferguson has won the European Cup-Winners' Cup twice, with Aberdeen in 1983 and with United in 1991, a feat equalled only by Johan Cruyff as manager of Ajax Amsterdam and Barcelona.

⚽ United won the 1991 Cup-Winners' Cup without losing a single match, compared with one defeat in the 1968 European Cup run.

⚽ Before 1990, United had won only once in nine away games in the European Cup-Winners' Cup. Yet in winning the 1990–91 contest they won all five away matches, including the final.

⚽ With their 100 per cent away record in the 1991 Cup Winners' Cup, United became the first team ever to win one of the three main European trophies by winning each of their away matches. Bayern Munich emulated this feat in winning the 1996 UEFA Cup.

{·} Seven of the seventeen goals United scored in winning the 1991 Cup-Winners' Cup came from defenders – Steve Bruce (4), Clayton Blackmore (2) and Gary Pallister (1).

{·} Arguably Steve Bruce could also claim a fifth strike with United's first goal against Barcelona in the final which was officially credited to Mark Hughes. Bruce's header was already certain to cross the line when Hughes followed up and unnecessarily gave the ball a finishing touch.

{·} In its 39-year life the European Cup-Winners' Cup came to England a record eight times, with seven different clubs – Tottenham Hotspur, West Ham United, Manchester City, Chelsea (twice), Everton, United and Arsenal.

{·} In three successive United games in the 1990–91 Cup Winners' Cup, and in four games out of five, opposing players were sent off – in both legs against Montpellier of France, in the away game against Legia Warsaw and then against Barcelona in the final.

EUROPEAN PLAYER RECORDS

{·} The United players to make most appearances in all main European competitions have been:

Bill Foulkes	1956–69	52 apps
Denis Irwin	1990–99	46 apps
Bobby Charlton	1957–69	45 apps
Peter Schmeichel	1991–99	43 apps
Gary Pallister	1990–98	41 apps
Tony Dunne	1963–69	40 apps

⚽ United's leading scorers in all main European competitions are:

Denis Law	1963–69	28 goals
Bobby Charlton	1957–69	22 goals
David Herd	1963–68	14 goals
Dennis Viollet	1956–58	13 goals
Andy Cole	1996–99	11 goals
Tommy Taylor	1956–58	11 goals
George Best	1964–69	11 goals
John Connelly	1964–66	11 goals

⚽ Dennis Viollet's 13 goals came in just 12 matches, while Denis Law scored his 28 goals in only 33 games in Europe.

WORLD CLUB CHAMPIONSHIP

⚽ Willie Morgan's goal in the home draw with Estudiantes in the 1968 World Club Championship is the only time a British club has even managed to score in six English and Scottish attempts at the title.

EUROPEAN FOOTBALLER OF THE YEAR

⚽ Three United players have been elected European Footballer of the Year – Denis Law in 1964, Bobby Charlton in 1966 and George Best in 1968. The only other winner with a British club was Stanley Matthews, with Blackpool in 1956, though Kevin Keegan won the title twice while playing for SV Hamburg.

⚽ Until Ronaldo won the trophy in 1997, George Best was the youngest-ever European Footballer of the Year, having won in 1968 at the age of 22.

3 REDS IN THE FA CUP

FA CUP WINS

⚽ United have now won the FA Cup a record ten times, two more than the next best team, Tottenham Hotspur, on eight. Arsenal and Aston Villa have won the trophy seven times. United's FA Cup final wins were:

1909	1–0	v. Bristol City
1948	4–2	v. Blackpool
1963	3–1	v. Leicester City
1977	2–1	v. Liverpool
1983	4–0	v. Brighton and Hove Albion (after 2–2 draw)
1985	1–0	v. Everton
1990	1–0	v. Crystal Palace (after 3–3 draw)
1994	4–0	v. Chelsea
1996	1–0	v. Liverpool
1999	2–0	v. Newcastle United

⚽ United have appeared in a record fifteen FA Cup finals compared with Arsenal and Newcastle United who have both appeared thirteen times. The Reds' losing finals were:

1957	1–2	v. Aston Villa
1958	0–2	v. Bolton Wanderers
1976	0–1	v. Southampton
1979	2–3	v. Arsenal
1995	0–1	v. Everton

⚽ In 1996 United became only the sixth side in history – and the third team this century – to reach the FA Cup final in three successive years. The Wanderers, Blackburn Rovers, West Bromwich Albion, Arsenal and Everton are the other clubs to have achieved this. No team has yet reached four consecutive FA Cup finals.

⚽ United are the only club to have appeared in an FA Cup final in each of the six decades since the Second World War.

SEMI-FINALS

⚽ United's twenty-two FA Cup semi-finals are surpassed only by Everton with twenty-three.

⚽ United have played in a record eleven FA Cup semi-final replays – in 1949, 1958, 1965, 1970 (twice), 1979, 1985, 1990, 1994, 1996 and 1999. The abolition of semi-final replays from 2000 onwards means this record is unlikely to be beaten.

⚽ For five successive years – from 1962 to 1966 – United reached the FA Cup semi-finals, but 1963 was the only year they went on to win the Cup.

⚽ Bobby Charlton played in eight FA Cup semi-finals – in 1957, 1958, 1962, 1963, 1964, 1965, 1966 and 1970 – which is probably an all-time record. These eight ties required a total of twelve matches to resolve them.

⚽ United have won all of their last ten FA Cup semi-final ties – in 1976, 1977, 1979, 1983, 1985, 1990, 1994, 1995, 1996 and 1999. Including replays, the Reds have been unbeaten in their last sixteen FA Cup semi-final matches.

⚽ In each of their seven FA Cup semi-finals between 1979 and 1996, United triumphed after being a goal down. They made come-backs against Liverpool in 1979, Arsenal in 1983, Liverpool again in 1985, Oldham Althletic in both 1990 and 1994, Crystal Palace in 1995 and Chelsea in 1996.

United avoided falling behind to Arsenal in the two 1999 semi-final matches, but did suffer a penalty award against them in injury time of the replay. Had Peter Schmeichel not saved the penalty, Arsenal would almost certainly have won the tie. Instead United went on to win 2–1.

⚽ The crowd of 17,987 for the 1995 replay against Crystal Palace was the lowest attendance at an FA Cup semi-final since the war.

RESULTS

⚽ United's best FA Cup victories are:

8–0	v. Yeovil Town (h)	12 February 1949
7–1	v. Brentford (h)	14 January 1928
8–2	v. Northampton Town (a)	7 February 1970
5–0	v. Huddersfield Town (h)	4 March 1963

⚽ Their worst FA Cup defeats are:

1–7	v. Burnley (a)	13 February 1901
2–7	v. Sheffield Wednesday (h)	1 February 1961

⚽ United's best FA Cup sequence was between January 1994 and April 1995, when they won eleven successive ties.
⚽ The best unbeaten run in the FA Cup was thirteen games, in 1948 and 1949, and again in 1994 and 1995.
⚽ The worst FA Cup sequence was three third-round defeats in 1932, 1933 and 1934. The worst home sequence ran from 1929 to 1935, during which United failed to win a single FA Cup game at Old Trafford.
⚽ In February 1992 United became the first top-division side to lose an FA Cup tie on penalties: 4–2 at home to Southampton in the fourth round.

⚽ United's most frequent FA Cup victims are Chelsea and Liverpool – both knocked out eight times. The Reds defeated Chelsea in the FA Cup in 1908, 1963, 1979, 1988, 1994, 1996, 1998 and 1999 and on four of those occasions United went on to win the cup. Between 1996 and 1999 United were the only side to beat Chelsea in the FA Cup, as the London club lifted the cup in 1997 and United knocked them out in the other three seasons.

⚽ United beat Liverpool in the FA Cup in 1903, 1948, 1960, 1977, 1979, 1985, 1996 and 1999, and in five of those seasons United then won the competition. Liverpool have only beaten United twice in the FA Cup, the last time in 1921.

⚽ Tottenham Hotspur, Everton and Sheffield Wednesday have defeated United the most often in the FA Cup – five times each.

FINAL MEDALS

⚽ Bryan Robson is the only player this century to have captained three FA Cup-winning sides – in 1983, 1985 and 1990.

⚽ Martin Buchan is the only man to have captained a team which won the Scottish Cup (Aberdeen, in 1970) as well as one which won the FA Cup (United, in 1977).

⚽ Seven United players have won three FA Cup winners' medals with the club:

Arthur Albiston (1977, 1983 & 1985)

Bryan Robson (1983, 1985 & 1990)

Mark Hughes (1985, 1990 & 1994)

Gary Pallister (1990, 1994 & 1996)

Peter Schmeichel (1994, 1996 & 1999)

Roy Keane (1994, 1996 & 1999)

Ryan Giggs (1994, 1996 & 1999)

⚽ All of the above except Robson also appeared in one other FA Cup final for United on the losing side – Albiston in 1979, and Hughes, Pallister, Schmeichel, Keane and Giggs in 1995.

⚽ Only fourteen other players in the twentieth century won three FA Cup-winners' medals.

⚽ In 1997, when he won the cup with Chelsea, Mark Hughes became the only player in the twentieth century to gain four FA Cup medals.

⚽ Four United players are among the eight men to have appeared in five Wembley FA Cup finals:

Johnny Giles
   (1963 with United, 1965, 1970, 1972 & 1973 with Leeds)
Frank Stapleton
   (1978, 1979, 1980 with Arsenal; 1983 & 1985 with United)
Mark Hughes
   (1985, 1990, 1994 & 1995 with United; 1997 with Chelsea)
Roy Keane
   (1991 with Nottm Forest; 1994, 1995, 1996 & 1999 with United)

⚽ In 1999 Roy Keane became the youngest of the eight men to achieve this record.

⚽ Frank Stapleton won one FA Cup winners' medal playing against United – in 1979 – and two with United, in 1983 and 1985. Stapleton is the only player to have played and scored for two different teams in Wembley FA Cup finals (1979 and 1983).

⚽ Stan Crowther also played both against and for United in the FA Cup final, appearing for Aston Villa in 1957 and United in 1958.

⚽ Harold Halse won an FA Cup-winners' medal with United in 1909, and another with Aston Villa in 1913, before gaining a losers' medal with Chelsea in 1915.

⚽ The only other player to appear in the final for three different clubs also played for United. Ernie Taylor won at Wembley with Newcastle United in 1951 and with Blackpool in 1953, but lost with United in 1958.

⚽ Billy Meredith won an FA Cup-winners' medal with Manchester City in 1904, and a second with United in 1909.

⚽ Arthur Albiston in 1977 and Alan Davies in 1983 both made their FA Cup debuts in the final. In 1990 Les Sealey made his FA Cup debut for United in the Wembley replay, and became the only player to appear in the final while on loan from another club.

⚽ George Best is probably the most distinguished player in English football never to have appeared in an FA Cup final.

APPEARANCES

⚽ Bobby Charlton holds United's FA Cup appearance record with 79 games. He scored on his cup debut in the 1957 semi-final against Birmingham City, and played in 75 consecutive FA Cup matches for United between 1958 and 1973.

⚽ Charlton subsequently played four more FA Cup games for Preston North End, and his total of 83 FA Cup appearances is the third highest in history, behind Ian Callaghan (88) and Stanley Matthews (86).

⚽ Bill Foulkes's 61 FA Cup matches for United were all consecutive – between 9 January 1954 and 28 January 1967.

⚽ Shay Brennan had the misfortune to appear in four FA Cup semi-finals for United – in 1958, 1962, 1965 and 1966 – without ever playing in the final. He missed Wembley trips in both 1958 and 1963.

GOALS

⚽ On 6 January 1996, Denis Law was overtaken by Ian Rush

as the most prolific FA Cup goalscorer since the war. Law is now in second place with 41 FA Cup goals compared with Rush's 43. However, Law scored another 6 goals in one FA Cup match for Manchester City against Luton in 1961, but since the game was abandoned these goals do not count towards his official total.

⚽ In 1983 Norman Whiteside became the youngest player to score in an FA Cup final, at the age of 18 years and 18 days. The same season he also became the youngest to score in a League Cup final, at 17 years 323 days. Whiteside later scored the winning goal in the 1985 FA Cup final.

⚽ United have scored a record 31 goals in FA Cup finals, and have produced four goals in the final on three occasions. Together with the 1968 European Cup final and the 1996 Charity Shield, United have scored four goals at Wembley on five occasions:

1948	FAC	4–2 v. Blackpool
1968	ECC	4–1 v. Benfica
1983	FAC	4–0 v. Brighton and Hove Albion
1994	FAC	4–0 v Chelsea
1996	CS	4–0 v. Newcastle United

⚽ Only on six other occasions has any club managed to score four goals or more at Wembley in senior matches (excluding play-offs and the members' cups), and none of them has done so more than once.

⚽ Jack Rowley, David Herd, Bryan Robson (3), Norman Whiteside, Mark Hughes (3) and Eric Cantona (3) have all scored two goals or more in FA Cup finals for United.

⚽ The only two players since the war to score FA Cup semi-final hat-tricks were both with United – Stan Pearson in 1948, and Alex Dawson in 1958.

THE LUCK OF THE DRAW

⚽ United's most regular FA Cup opponents have been Liverpool, with whom they have been paired ten times.

⚽ United's most protracted tie in the FA Cup was against Small Heath (later Birmingham City) in 1903–04, which went to three replays and seven hours of football before United triumphed 3–1.

⚽ In the nine competitive seasons between 1938 and 1953, United were drawn against non-League sides four times in the FA Cup – Yeovil Town (1938 and 1948), Weymouth (1949) and Walthamstow Avenue (1953) – yet they have not met non-League opposition in forty-six seasons since then.

⚽ The Walthamstow Avenue team that forced United to a replay in 1953 contained the Essex and England cricketer Trevor Bailey.

⚽ United's FA Cup tie with Reading in January 1996 was the sixth time the two clubs had been drawn against each other in the FA Cup, though they have never met in the League.

⚽ In 1946 United beat Preston North End 1–0 in the FA Cup, but Preston still went through. Because there was no League competition that season, cup ties were played over two legs and Preston won the second game 3–1.

⚽ For four years out of five – 1958, 1960, 1961 and 1962 – United met Sheffield Wednesday in the FA Cup.

⚽ In 1965 United were drawn to meet Stoke City, Burnley and Wolverhampton Wanderers in the fourth, fifth and sixth rounds of the FA Cup, after fixtures against each side at home in the League the previous Saturday. They then played the semi-final at Hillsborough having visited Sheffield Wednesday there the week before.

⚽ Over three successive years – 1970, 1971 and 1972 – United were drawn against Middlesbrough in the FA Cup, and each tie went to a replay. In 1969, 1973 and 1974 they also met Middlesbrough in the League Cup.

◉ In three years out of four – 1983, 1985 and 1986 – United met West Ham United in the FA Cup.

◉ The only four meetings between United and Sheffield United in the FA Cup occurred over the space of just six years – in 1990, 1993, 1994 and 1995 – and each time the tie was in Sheffield. The three years in which United won – 1990, 1994 and 1995 – they went on to Wembley.

◉ United have met Crystal Palace only twice in the FA Cup – in the 1990 final and the 1994 semi-final – and won both times after a replay.

◉ Sunderland have had an astonishingly frustrating time against United in cup competitions. Over four pairings in the FA Cup the tie has always gone to a replay, and two re-plays in 1964. The only League Cup tie between the sides, in 1976, also generated two replays. In a dozen cup matches, Sunderland have taken the lead no fewer than twelve times, and United have pulled back on every occasion and eventu-ally gone on to win. United have yet to lose a cup tie against Sunderland.

◉ In January 1974 a programme was printed for an FA Cup replay involving United at Plymouth Argyle. Yet no replay was needed since United had won the tie at Old Trafford 1–0. Plymouth had printed the programme in advance as a precaution against power cuts during the three-day week.

GIANT-KILLERS

◉ Twice Norwich City have giant-killed United in the FA Cup – in 1959 and 1967. The first year United were League runners-up, the second they were champions.

◉ In five of the first seven seasons that United were League champions, they lost to lower-division sides in the FA Cup: Fulham (division two, 1908); West Ham United (non-League, 1911); Hull City (division two, 1952); Bristol Rovers (division three south, 1956) and Norwich City (division two, 1967). And in 1975, when United were second-division champions, they lost to third division Walsall.

⚽ The full list of post-war defeats by lower-division sides (from division two, unless stated) is:

1946–47	Nottingham Forest	(h)	0–2
1950–51	Birmingham City	(a)	0–1
1951–52	Hull City	(h)	0–2
1952–53	Everton	(a)	1–2
1955–56	Bristol Rovers (d3 south)	(a)	0–4
1958–59	Norwich City (d3)	(a)	0–3
1966–67	Norwich City	(h)	1–2
1970–71	Middlesbrough	(a)	1–2
1974–75	Walsall (d3)	(a)	2–3
1975–76	Southampton	(W)	0–1
1981–82	Watford	(a)	0–1
1983–84	Bournemouth	(a)	0–2

1909 WINNERS

⚽ United were lucky to win the Cup in 1909. In the quarter-final in March they were losing 1–0 at Burnley with 18 minutes to go. But then the match was abandoned because of a sudden snowstorm, and United went on to win both the replay and the Cup. In 1927 the referee who had abandoned the game at Burnley, Herbert Bamlett, became United's manager.

1948 WINNERS

⚽ 1948 was the only year a team has won the Cup after beating first-division opponents in every round. The achievement was all the more remarkable in that United didn't play a single match at home. Old Trafford was closed because of wartime bomb damage, and the team played 'home' ties at Huddersfield, Goodison Park and Maine Road.

⚽ United's 1948 victory was also notable in that they won each tie by two goals or more.

⚽ Jimmy Delaney's FA Cup medal in 1948 was part of a unique treble. He had already won a Scottish Cup medal with Glasgow Celtic in 1937, and later gained an Irish Cup medal with Derry City in 1954. He also won an FA of Ireland Cup finalists' medal with Cork Athletic in 1956.

1958 MUNICH FINAL

⚽ In 1958 Stan Crowther became the only FA Cup finalist to appear for two clubs in the competition in the same season. Crowther was transferred from Aston Villa to United an hour before the fifth-round game against Sheffield Wednesday. The FA waived their rule that players can appear for only one club in the Cup in any one season, out of sympathy for United following the Munich air disaster.

⚽ No member of the Bolton Wanderers side that beat United in the 1958 final had previously played for another club – the only time this has ever happened.

1963 WINNERS

⚽ In 1963 United played and won all their first four rounds of the FA Cup over twenty-seven days in March. Freezing weather conditions had led numerous ties to be postponed.

1977 WINNERS

⚽ Tommy Docherty's success in the 1977 FA Cup final over Liverpool was his last game as United manager. Six weeks later he resigned over his affair with Mary Brown, the wife of the United physiotherapist.

⚽ When David McCreery replaced Gordon Hill in the 1977 final it was the second successive year that Hill had been substituted by McCreery at Wembley.

⚽ McCreery also became the only teenager ever to appear in two FA Cup finals.

1983 WINNERS

⚽ United's 4–0 victory over Brighton & Hove Albion in the 1983 FA Cup final replay was the highest winning margin in a final since Bury beat Derby County 6–0 in 1903.

⚽ United also emulated Bury in scoring six goals in the final (counting the initial 2–2 draw). United won 4–0 in the final again in 1994, against Chelsea.

⚽ Alan Davies became the most inexperienced player ever to appear in an FA Cup final. Before the 1983 final against Brighton and the subsequent replay, he had played only three League games for United.

⚽ United reached the 1983 FA Cup semi-final without conceding a goal.

1985 WINNERS

⚽ United won the FA Cup in 1985 despite the sending-off of Kevin Moran, the only player ever dismissed in an FA Cup final.

⚽ The 1985 FA Cup win with United gave Gordon Strachan four cup medals in successive years, following Scottish Cup triumphs with Aberdeen in 1982, 1983 and 1984.

⚽ 1985 was the second time that United stopped a Merseyside Treble. In 1977 United had prevented Liverpool from adding the FA Cup to the League and European Cups, while in 1985 Everton had been trying to add the Cup to the League and European Cup-Winners' Cup.

⚽ United's 1985 final side boasted four players who have scored in two FA Cup finals: Frank Stapleton (1979 and 1983), Bryan Robson (1983 and 1990), Norman Whiteside (1983 and 1985) and Mark Hughes (1990 and 1994).

⚽ Between January 1981 and March 1986, United did not lose to a first-division club in the FA Cup. In the 1982 tournament they were defeated by second-division Watford, and in 1984 by third-division Bournemouth, while in 1983 and 1985 they won the Cup.

1990 WINNERS

⚽ United played every game in the 1990 competition on Sundays until the semi-final replay.

⚽ The three FA Cup semi-final games in 1990 – Crystal Palace's 4–3 win over Liverpool, and United's 3–3 draw with Oldham and subsequent 2–1 win – produced sixteen goals from sixteen different players. A further three players scored in the final, making nineteen different scorers in the 1990 FA Cup semi-finals and final.

⚽ Les Sealey's appearance in the 1990 final replay, when United won the cup, was only his third game for the club.

⚽ The 1990 team cost United £12 million, yet the winning goal was scored by a home-grown player, Lee Martin, who cost nothing.

⚽ Lee Martin was the first left-back to score a winning FA Cup final goal.

⚽ Lee Martin's strike in 1990 was only his second goal for United, and he never scored again for the club.

⚽ In 1990 Alex Ferguson became the only manager since the war to win both the FA Cup (which he was to win again in 1994, 1996 and 1999) and the Scottish Cup (which he had lifted with Aberdeen in 1982, 1983, 1984 and 1986).

⚽ Just as in 1948, United played no games at home during the 1990 tournament, but unlike 1948 they were not even *drawn* to play at home.

⚽ Three major knock-out trophies went to Old Trafford in 1990: while United won the FA Cup, Lancashire County Cricket Club won both the Benson & Hedges Cup and the NatWest Trophy.

1994 WINNERS

⚽ With his two penalties in 1994, Eric Cantona became the first Frenchman to score in an FA Cup final.

⚽ With his goal in the 1994 final, Mark Hughes became the only player to score at Wembley in four different club matches in one season. Hughes had already scored in the Charity Shield, the League Cup final, and the FA Cup semi-final.

⚽ The 1994 FA Cup final was the last occasion on which that year's United Double team all played together.

⚽ In 1994 Gary Walsh achieved the unusual distinction of winning an FA Cup winners' medal with United despite never playing for the club at any time in the FA Cup. He won his medal through being named as one of the United's three substitutes for the 1994 final, but was never required in the game. Nor had Walsh appeared earlier in United's cup campaign that season, and remarkably, despite 63 appearances for the club in nine years, not once did he ever play for the club in the competition.

1996 WINNERS

⚽ In scoring against Liverpool in 1996, Eric Cantona became only the fourth player in history to hit the winning goal in two FA Cup finals.

⚽ Eric Cantona also became the first man from outside the British Isles to captain an FA Cup-winning team.

⚽ When Gary Neville came on as substitute two minutes from the end of the 1996 final, he and Philip Neville became the first brothers to play in an FA Cup-winning side since Jimmy and Brian Greenhoff with United in 1977.

1999 WINNERS

⚽ United's 1999 campaign was arguably the toughest ever endured by an FA Cup winning side. It involved all six teams that had taken part in the three previous FA Cup finals – Liverpool (who lost to United in 1996); Chelsea and Middlesbrough (1997); and Arsenal and Newcastle United (1998).

⚽ When Roy Keane was sent off in the FA Cup semi-final replay against Arsenal, it was the second time he had been sent off in an FA Cup semi-final replay at Villa Park, following his dismissal against Crystal Palace in 1995. David Elleray was the referee on both occasions.

⚽ Raimond van der Gouw emulated Gary Walsh's achievement of winning an FA Cup winners' medal despite never having appeared in the FA Cup for United. Unlike Walsh, van der Gouw has never played in the FA Cup for any other team either. Yet Denis Irwin, who was suspended for the 1999 final, was deprived of a medal despite playing in all but one of United's other FA Cup matches that season.

4 REDS IN THE LEAGUE CUP

⚽ The League Cup is by far United's least fruitful domestic competition. United have won the trophy just once in 32 attempts.

⚽ Former United manager Ron Atkinson has twice defeated his old club in the League Cup final, as manager of Sheffield Wednesday in 1991 and of Aston Villa in 1994.

⚽ Between 1990 and 1994, United were defeated in the League Cup only by teams managed by Ron Atkinson – Sheffield Wednesday in 1991, and Aston Villa in 1993 and 1994. In 1992 United won the Cup.

⚽ Bryan Robson, with 51 matches, has played the most League Cup games for United.

⚽ Brian McClair is United's highest League Cup scorer with 21 goals.

⚽ In 1987 McClair scored in each of his first four League Cup games for United.

⚽ In reaching the 1991 League Cup final, United beat the sides then placed first (Arsenal) and second (Liverpool) in the first division, but lost to a second-division side, Sheffield Wednesday, at Wembley.

⚽ In the second round of the 1990–91 League Cup, United played Halifax Town, then bottom of the fourth division. Halifax had yet to score in the League that season, yet scored in each leg against United.

⚽ United's 6–2 win at Arsenal in the League Cup fourth round in November 1990 was notable for several

reasons:

◉ It was Arsenal's heaviest defeat at Highbury since Sheffield United won by the same score in 1921, 69 years before.

◉ Arsenal had conceded only seven other goals in 17 previous games that season.

◉ It ended Arsenal's unbeaten run in the 1990–91 campaign, United having already ended similar runs by Liverpool and Crystal Palace.

◉ Lee Sharpe scored a hat-trick, having scored only three other goals in 61 previous appearances for United.

◉ The victory was achieved in the absence of both club captain Bryan Robson and his usual deputy Neil Webb.

◉ It meant that United had played eleven cup rounds in the 1990 calendar year, and sixteen cup games, without losing once.

◉ It was United's best-ever away score in the League Cup.

◉ Lee Sharpe scored six goals in seven appearances in the 1990–91 League Cup, yet by the end of the season had scored only four other goals in 84 other League and cup games for United.

◉ Paul Ince scored twice in his second match for United in a League Cup tie at Portsmouth in 1989, but it was 70 games before he scored again in any competition.

◉ United's best League Cup wins are:

7–2	v. Newcastle United (h)	27 October 1976
6–2	v. Arsenal (a)	28 November 1990

◉ United's best League Cup win over two legs was 7–0 (4–0 (h) and 3–0 (a)), against Burnley in the second round in 1984–85.

⚽ United's worst League Cup defeats are:

1–5	v. Blackpool (a)	14 September 1966
0–3	v. Everton (h)	1 December 1976
0–3	v. Tottenham Hotspur (h)	25 October 1989
0–3	v. York City (h)	20 September 1995

⚽ Of the three 3–0 defeats at home, that against York City was by far the worst, as York were two divisions below United and only just avoided relegation that season.

⚽ United have suffered 'giant-killings' in the League Cup on nine occasions, and six times by teams two divisions below them:

1960–61	Bradford City (d3)	(a) 1–2
1970–71	Aston Villa (d3)	(h) 1–1; (a) 1–2; agg: 2–3
1972–73	Bristol Rovers (d3)	(h) 1–2
1973–74	Middlesbrough (d2)	(h) 0–1
1978–79	Watford (d3)	(h) 1–2
1983–84	Oxford United (d3)	(a) 1–2
1990–91	Sheffield Wednesday (d2)	(W) 0–1
1995–96	York City (new d2)	(h) 0–3; (a) 3–1; agg: 3–4
1997–98	Ipswich Town (new d1)	(a) 0–2

⚽ United's defeat by second-division Sheffield Wednesday in the 1991 League Cup final was the second time they had been beaten by a lower-division side at Wembley, following the loss to Southampton in the 1976 FA Cup final. Arsenal are the only other club to have lost twice to lower-division teams at Wembley.

⚽ United were not only unbeaten in winning the 1991–92 League Cup, but they also became the first team to be unbeaten during open play in both domestic cups in the same season. They were eliminated from the 1992 FA Cup only after a penalty shoot-out against Southampton.

⚽ The League champions in both 1990–91 and 1991–92, Arsenal and Leeds United, could both boast unbeaten home League records. Yet in the League Cup United brought them down to earth, winning 6–2 at Arsenal in 1990–91 and 3–1 at Leeds in 1991–92 (as well as beating Leeds 1–0 in the FA Cup).

5 RED FACES

MOST GAMES

⚽ The twenty players with the most appearances in all first class competitions are:

		Seasons	Games	Goals
1	Bobby Charlton	1956–73	759*	249
2	Bill Foulkes	1952–69	688*	9
3	Alex Stepney	1966–78	539*	2
4	Tony Dunne	1960–73	535*	2
5	Joe Spence	1919–33	510	168
6	Arthur Albiston	1974–88	485*	7
7	George Best	1963–74	470*	179
=8	Mark Hughes	1983–95	468*	163
	Brian McClair	1987–98	468*	127
10	Bryan Robson	1981–94	460*	99
11	Martin Buchan	1972–82	456*	4
12	Jack Silcock	1919–34	449	2
13	Gary Pallister	1989–98	437*	15
14	Denis Irwin	1990–99	434*	28
15	Jack Rowley	1937–55	424*	211
16	Sammy McIlroy	1971–81	419*	71
17	Steve Bruce	1987–96	415*	53
18	Denis Law	1962–73	404*	237
19	Lou Macari	1973–83	401*	97
20	Peter Schmeichel	1991–99	398*	1

* Includes Charity Shield, World Club Championship and European Super Cup

> ⚽ Bobby Charlton played for United 759 times between 1956 and 1973. He also played a record 606 League games for the club, including two as substitute.

⚽ The twenty players with the most league appearances are:

		Seasons	Games	Goals
1	Bobby Charlton	1956–73	606	199
2	Bill Foulkes	1952–69	566	7
3	Joe Spence	1919–33	481	158
4	Alex Stepney	1966–78	433	2
5	Jack Silcock	1919–34	423	2
6	Tony Dunne	1960–73	414	2
7	Jack Rowley	1937–55	380	182
8	Arthur Albiston	1974–88	379	6
9	Martin Buchan	1972–82	376	4
10	George Best	1963–74	361	137
11	Brian McClair	1987–98	355	88
12	Allenby Chilton	1939–54	353	3
=13	Mark Hughes	1983–95	345	120
	Bryan Robson	1981–94	345	74
15	Sammy McIlroy	1971–81	342	57
16	Gary Pallister	1989–98	337	12
17	Lou Macari	1973–83	329	78
18	Steve Coppell	1975–83	322	54
19	Stan Pearson	1937–53	315	128
20	Nobby Stiles	1960–71	311	17

⚽ Billy Meredith has the distinction of having played more than 300 League games for both Manchester clubs – 366 for City and 303 for United.

BRIEFEST APPEARANCES

⚽ The shortest United careers have been:

Michael Twiss* (sub)	11 mins	v. Barnsley (FAC)(a)	25 Feb. 1998
Alex Notman* (sub)	18 mins	v. Tottenham (LC)(a)	2 Dec. 1998
Paul Wratten (sub)	6 mins	v. Wimbledon (h)	2 Apr. 1991
(sub)	17 mins	v. Crystal Palace (a)	11 May 1991
Jonathan Clark (sub)	30 mins	v. Sunderland (h)	10 Nov. 1976
Danny			
Higginbotham* (sub)	30 mins	v. Barnsley (a)	10 May 1998
Jimmy Kelly (sub)	35 mins	v. Wolves (h)	20 Dec. 1975
Ronnie Wallwork*			
(sub)	26 mins	v. Barnsley (h)	25 Oct. 1997
(sub)	12 mins	v. Nottm F (LC)(h)	11 Nov. 1998
Graeme Tomlinson			
(sub)	25 mins	v. Port Vale (LC)(h)	5 Oct. 1994
(sub)	17 mins	v. Newcastle (LC)(a)	26 Oct. 1994
Anto Whelan (sub)	43 mins	v. Southampton (h)	29 Nov. 1980
Peter Beardsley	45 mins	v. Bournem'th (LC)(h)	6 Oct. 1982
Pat McGibbon (so)	51 mins	v. York City (LC)(h)	20 Sept. 1995
Neil Whitworth	54 mins	v. Southampton (a)	16 Mar. 1991

*still on United's books (July 1999)

CONSECUTIVE GAMES

⚽ The longest run of consecutive League games is 206 by Steve Coppell, between 15 January 1977 and 7 November 1981.

⚽ Jack Rowley had the longest time-span in the United first team. There was a gap of 17 years and 98 days between his first appearance, at home to Sheffield Wednesday on 23 October 1937, and his last, in the FA Cup at Manchester City on 29 January 1955.

◉ Clayton Blackmore wore every outfield shirt for United between 1984 and 1994, from number 2 to number 14.

◉ Between 1937 and 1953 Johnny Carey played for United in every position, including goal, except outside-left. He played for the Republic of Ireland and Northern Ireland in six positions.

◉ Walter Cartwright played in every position except outside-right between 1895 and 1904, including two appearances in goal.

UNCHANGED TEAMS

◉ The team that played the first match of the 1956–57 season also appeared on 14 December 1957, sixteen months later.

◉ In both the 1956–57 and 1957–58 seasons, United fielded the same side for the first nine League games.

◉ In the 1948–49, 1967–68 and 1979–80 seasons, ten of the players who turned out for the first League game also appeared in the final match.

◉ In the 1957–58 Munich season, only two players – Bill Foulkes and Dennis Viollet – played in both the first and last League matches, while Foulkes managed to appear in all forty-two games. In each of the 1931–32 and 1932–33 seasons, only three players played in both the first and last League games.

◉ Between 6 December 1975 and 9 March 1976, United's starting line-up (except for substitutes) remained unchanged for thirteen consecutive League matches and five FA Cup games – eighteen matches in all.

MOST TEAM CHANGES

◉ At home to Burnley in April 1957, United fielded eight reserves, and nine of the players had not appeared in the previous first-team game two days before. Matt Busby was resting the first team in preparation for the European Cup semi-final against Real Madrid three days later. United still beat Burnley 2–0.

⚽ United's starting line-up at Derby County on 18 October 1997 was a totally different eleven from the team which began the League Cup game at Ipswich four days before.

⚽ Similarly, United's starting line-up against Nottingham Forest in the League Cup on 11 November 1998 was a completely different team from that which began the League game against Newcastle three days earlier.

⚽ Not surprisingly, of the team that played Red Star Belgrade the day before the Munich disaster, only two – Harry Gregg and Bill Foulkes – played in the subsequent game, against Sheffield Wednesday in the FA Cup two weeks later.

MOST PLAYERS IN A SEASON

⚽ The most players used in one season by United was 38 in 1933–34, 7 short of the League-record 45 fielded by Darwen in 1898–99.

⚽ Over the three seasons from 1931–32 to 1933–34, United used 62 players in League games.

⚽ United needed only 19 players in 1964–65, and only 18 in the League – 4 more than the League record held jointly by Liverpool and Aston Villa.

⚽ The most appearances in a season by a United player is 62 (including one game as substitute in each case) by both Denis Irwin and Gary Pallister in 1993–94.

YOUNGEST PLAYERS

⚽ United's youngest post-war player was goalkeeper David

Gaskell when he appeared as substitute for Ray Wood in the
Charity Shield against Manchester City on 24 October 1956
at the age of 16 years and 19 days. Many players' ages from
the club's early history are not recorded, but Gaskell is probably the youngest United player of all time.

⚽ United's youngest post-war League player was Jeff
Whitefoot when he appeared at home to Portsmouth on 15
April 1950 aged 16 years and 105 days. It seems likely that
Whitefoot is the youngest League player in United history.

⚽ The full list of post-war players to appear before their
seventeenth birthday is:

David Gaskell	Man. City (CS)(a)	24 Oct. 1956	16 y, 19 d
Jeff Whitefoot	Portsmouth (h)	15 Apr. 1950	16 y, 105 d
Duncan Edwards	Cardiff City (h)	4 Apr. 1953	16 y, 185 d
Willie Anderson	Burnley (h)	28 Dec. 1963	16 y, 338 d
Norman Whiteside	Brighton (a)	24 Apr. 1982	16 y, 352 d

⚽ Three other players appeared for United in friendlies before they were seventeen:

Sammy McIlroy	Bohemians (a)	21 Jan. 1971	16 y, 172 d
Roy Morton	Mallorca (a)	18 May 1972	16 y, 202 d
Ian Moir	Shamrock Rovers (a)	5 Apr. 1960	16 y, 280 d

⚽ Peter Coyne was only seventeen when he made his debut
for United. He played just one full game for the club in
1975–76, plus one substitute appearance, and scored once.
He then left League soccer, but returned later with Crewe
Alexandra and Swindon Town.

YOUNGEST TEAM

⚽ United's youngest-ever team was almost certainly that

which played West Bromwich Albion at home on 27 August 1955: the average age was 22 years, 106 days. The team was Wood, Foulkes, Byrne, Whitefoot, Jones, Edwards, Webster, Blanchflower, Lewis, Viollet and Scanlon.

✪ The second-youngest side – just ten days older – appeared at Bolton Wanderers in October 1960. Its average age was 22 years, 116 days. The team was Gregg, Setters, Brennan, Stiles, Foulkes, Nicholson, Moir, Giles, Dawson, Charlton and Scanlon.

✪ The above teams had two and four teenagers respectively, but in the League Cup at Port Vale in October 1994 United fielded six players under twenty – Chris Casper, John O'Kane, Nicky Butt, Keith Gillespie, David Beckham and Paul Scholes. The team's average age was 22 years, 243 days.

OLDEST PLAYERS

✪ Billy Meredith was 46 years and 281 days old when he played against Derby County on 7 May 1921 – almost three times as old as David Gaskell on his debut. Meredith was eight years older than the next-oldest known United player, Frank Mann. Three years after this final appearance for United, Meredith played in an FA Cup semi-final for Manchester City and became the oldest player in FA Cup history.

✪ Among United's oldest-ever players are:

Billy Meredith	Derby County (h)	7 May 1921	46 y, 281 d
Frank Mann	Sheffield Wed. (a)	16 Nov. 1929	38 y, c.240 d
Jack Warner	Newcastle U. (a)	22 Apr. 1950	38 y, 213 d
Thomas Jones	Bradford P.A. (a)	11 Dec. 1937	38 y, 5 d
Teddy Partridge	Aston Villa (h)	1 Jan. 1929	37 y, 323 d
George Livingstone	Aston Villa (h)	14 Mar. 1914	37 y, 313 d
Clarence Hilditch	Nottingham F. (h)	30 Jan. 1932	37 y, 243 d
Bill Foulkes	Southampton (h)	16 Aug. 1969	37 y, 223 d

| Bryan Robson | Coventry City (h) 8 May 1994 | 37 y, 117 d |
| Jack Hacking | Norwich City (a) 2 Feb. 1935 | 37 y, 42 d |

◉ United's oldest post-war player, Jack Warner, on his appearance at Newcastle United in April 1950, was replacing Jeff Whitefoot who had been United's *youngest* post-war player in the previous game.

◉ Ten post-war players have been thirty-five or older:

Jack Warner	Newcastle U. (a)	22 Apr. 1950	38 y, 213 d
Bill Foulkes	Southampton (h)	16 Aug. 1969	37 y, 223 d
Bryan Robson	Coventry City (h)	8 May 1994	37 y, 117 d
Les Sealey	Aston Villa (W) LC Final	27 Mar. 1994	36 y, 179 d
Allenby Chilton	Wolves (h)	23 Feb. 1955	36 y, 160 d
Jimmy Delaney	Chelsea (a)	11 Nov. 1950	36 y, 69 d
Raimond van der Gouw	Sheffield Wed. (h)	17 Apr. 1999	36 y, 24 d
Bobby Charlton	Chelsea (a)	28 Apr. 1973	35 y, 199 d
Peter Schmeichel	Bayern Munich (n) ECC Final	26 May 1999	35 y, 189 d
Steve Bruce	Leeds United (h)	17 Apr. 1996	35 y, 108 d

◉ The Scottish international centre-half Neil McBain played for United in the early 1920s. A generation later he became the oldest player in League history. On 15 March 1947, while manager of New Brighton, he turned out as emergency goalkeeper for his side at the age of 51 years and 120 days.

TALLEST AND SHORTEST

◉ It's not known for sure who has been United's tallest-ever player, but Gordon McQueen, Gary Pallister and Peter Schmeichel were all 6 feet 4 inches (1.93 m) in height.

⚽ Again, one cannot be certain who United's shortest-ever player was, but Warren Bradley, Bernard Donaghy, Terry Gibson, Ernie Taylor and Billy Wrigglesworth were all only 5 feet 4 inches (1.63 m) tall.

CAPTAINS

⚽ United club captains have included:

1882	E. Thomas
c.1883–1887	Sam Black
c.1887–1890	Jack Powell
1892–1893	Joe Cassidy
c.1894	James McNaught
c.1896–1903	Harry Stafford
c.1904–1905	Jack Peddie
c.1905–1912	Charlie Roberts
1912–1913	George Stacey
1913	Dick Duckworth
1914	George Hunter
1914–1915	Patrick O'Connell
c.1922–1928	Frank Barson
c.1928–1931	Jack Wilson
1931–1932	George McLachlan
1932	Louis Page
c.1935–1939	Jimmy Brown
1945–1953	Johnny Carey
1953–1954	Stan Pearson
1954–1955	Allenby Chilton
1955–1958	Roger Byrne
1958–1959	Bill Foulkes
1959–1960	Dennis Viollet
1960–1962	Maurice Setters
1962–1964	Noel Cantwell

1964–1967	Denis Law
1967–1973	Bobby Charlton
1973	George Graham
1973–1975	Willie Morgan
1975–1982	Martin Buchan
1982	Ray Wilkins
1982–1994	Bryan Robson
1994–1996	Steve Bruce
1996–1997	Eric Cantona
1997–	Roy Keane

⚽ Others who have captained the team for odd games, or parts of games, include Hugh McLenahan, George Roughton, Jack Warner, Charlie Mitten, Ray Wood, Johnny Berry, Ernie Taylor, Albert Quixall, David Herd, John Connelly, Pat Crerand, Ian Ure, Lou Macari, Brian Greenhoff, Stewart Houston, Sammy McIlroy, Steve Coppell, Arthur Albiston, Kevin Moran, Frank Stapleton, Mike Duxbury, Norman Whiteside, Brian McClair, Neil Webb, Mike Phelan, Paul Ince, Gary Pallister, Denis Irwin, Peter Schmeichel, Gary Neville, Henning Berg, Jaap Stam and David May.

⚽ Bryan Robson was club captain for almost twelve years, and thus the longest-serving skipper in United history. When he left the job in 1994, his predecessor, Ray Wilkins, was still playing League soccer.

⚽ Martin Buchan was made captain for his home debut against Everton on 8 March 1972.

⚽ Five of the nine most recent United captains have had brothers who played League football – Jackie Charlton, George Buchan, Graham Wilkins, Gary Robson and Joel Cantona.

BLACK PLAYERS

⚽ The first black player to appear for United was Dennis

Walker, who played just one game, at Nottingham Forest on 20 May 1963. The full list of of the 15 blacks to play for United, in order of appearance, is as follows:

Dennis Walker	1963
Remi Moses	1981–1988
Paul McGrath	1982–1989
Laurie Cunningham	1983
Garth Crooks	1983–1984
Viv Anderson	1987–1990
Paul Ince	1989–1995
Danny Wallace	1989–1993
Ryan Giggs	1991–
Paul Parker	1991–1996
Dion Dublin	1992–1994
John O'Kane	1995–1998
Andy Cole	1995–
Wes Brown	1998–
Dwight Yorke	1998–

⚽ Paul Ince was the first black player to captain United.

BROTHERS

⚽ The following sets of brothers have appeared together for United:

Roger and Jack Doughty	26 games	1889–91
Fred and Harry Erentz	4 games	1898
James and John Hodge	1 game	Dec. 1913
Martin and George Buchan	4 games	Sept. to Oct. 1973
Jimmy and Brian Greenhoff	80 games	Nov. 1976 to May 1979
Gary and Philip Neville	107 games	May 1995 onwards

⚽ Gary and Phil Neville have now played together for United 107 times, more often than any previous set of brothers.

⚽ The only occasion on which two brothers have scored in the same game for United – or rather Newton Heath – occurred in the old Football Alliance, before the club was admitted to the Football League. In April 1890, Jack and Roger Doughty both scored against Small Heath (the future Birmingham City).

⚽ Although James Hodge played 86 games for United between 1910 and 1919, and his brother John appeared 30 times between 1913 and 1915, they played together in the first team only once, against Sheffield Wednesday in December 1913.

⚽ On 2 April 1898 Harry Erentz played at left-back. Six days later his brother Fred filled the position, before it reverted to Harry in the next match.

⚽ In 1996 Gary and Philip Neville became the first brothers to win the Double since the Cowan brothers with Aston Villa in 1897, and the first to win the League since Denis and Leslie Compton with Arsenal in 1948.

⚽ The future United player Danny Wallace played with his two brothers, Rod and Ray, in the same team for Southampton.

⚽ Bobby and Jackie Charlton (Leeds United) played together 28 times for England, and both won World Cup medals in 1966. They also share the distinction of being the only pair of brothers to have held the record for most appearances for their respective clubs – Bobby with United, and Jackie with Leeds.

⚽ Jackie and Danny Blanchflower (Tottenham Hotspur) played together for Northern Ireland on 12 occasions.

RELATIONS

⚽ Darren Ferguson is the son of the United manager, Alex Ferguson.

⚽ Don Gibson became Matt Busby's son-in-law when he married the manager's daughter, Sheena.

⚽ Charlie Mitten is Albert Scanlon's uncle.

⚽ Nobby Stiles married Johnny Giles's sister.

⚽ David Herd's father Alec also played League football. In May 1951 both Herds played in the same match for Stockport County – one of only two occasions on which father and son have played together in the same League team.

SUBSTITUTES

⚽ United's first League substitute, though not used, was Noel Cantwell at home to Sheffield Wednesday on 21 August 1965.

⚽ The first United League substitute to be brought on to the field was John Fitzpatrick, for Denis Law at Tottenham Hotspur on 16 October 1965.

⚽ Ron Davies appeared as substitute ten times in 1974–75 without ever making a full appearance.

⚽ United's most frequently used substitute has been Brian McClair with 73 appearances from the bench, followed by Paul Scholes with 58, and David McCreery with 52.

⚽ Since substitutes were introduced, George Best has made the most appearances, 466, without ever appearing as a substitute, and Martin Buchan 455 appearances. Even Bobby Charlton was a substitute twice.

⚽ Against Eintracht Frankfurt in a friendly in Los Angeles in May 1970, Francis Burns started the game, and was then replaced by Steve James, but then Burns in turn came on as substitute for Paul Edwards. Burns was replaced for a second time by Willie Watson, but then came on for a third spell in place of Pat Crerand.

⚽ 14 players have been named as substitute for the United first team without ever getting a game. They are, in order of non-appearance: Peter McBride, Nicky Murphy, Eric Young, Peter Bodak, Fraser Digby, Craig Lawton, Brian Carey, Paul Sixsmith, David Johnson, Tony Coton, Paul Gibson, Nick Culkin, Paul Teather and Ryan Ford. (Culkin, Teather and Ford are still on the books – July 1999).

⚽ When Arsenal brought on substitute Brian Hornsby against United at Highbury in August 1973, he played for only 3 seconds before the final whistle.

GRADUATES

⚽ At least seven graduates have played for United:

Warren Bradley	General Studies, Durham University
Mike Pinner	Law, Cambridge University
Alan Gowling	Economics, Manchester University
Steve Coppell	Economics, Liverpool University
Gary Bailey	Physics, Witts University, South Africa
Kevin Moran	Commerce, University College, Dublin
Raimond van der Gouw	Physical Education

⚽ Joe Hanrahan also graduated from University College, Dublin, but never played in the first team.

⚽ Brian McClair read Mathematics at Glasgow, and Nicky Wood went to Manchester University, but neither graduated.

DEBUTS

⚽ On 1 January 1907 Herbert Burgess, Sandy Turnbull, Jimmy Bannister and Billy Meredith all made their debuts for United after being transferred from Manchester City. Each had been found guilty of offences committed while playing for City in 1906, and their suspensions had just expired.

⚽ Billy Redman was picked for the first team at the age of eighteen in 1946, but the game was postponed. It was another four years before he made his debut, in November 1950.

⚽ Bobby Charlton scored two goals on his debut on 6 October 1956 – appropriately, against Charlton Athletic. Four months later, in only his sixth match, he scored a hat-trick against Charlton at Old Trafford.

⚽ Albert Pape travelled to Old Trafford with his team, Clapton Orient, on 7 February 1925, but was actually transferred to United an hour before the kick-off. He then played in the match and scored for United.

⚽ Three players have made just one appearance for United and scored: R. Stephenson against Rotherham Town (h) in 1896, Bill Bainbridge against Accrington Stanley (h) in the FA Cup in 1946 and Albert Kinsey against Chester (h) in the FA Cup in 1965.

⚽ Dion Dublin had an eventful start to his United career in 1992. Having made his first-team debut in a friendly in Dublin of all places, he scored on his away League debut at Southampton, and then broke his leg on his Old Trafford debut against Crystal Palace.

⚽ Roy Keane wore four different types of shirt on his first four appearances for United in July and August 1993: all blue, in a friendly against Arsenal in Johannesburg; yellow and green in a friendly against Benfica; all black in a friendly against Celtic; and red and white, against Arsenal again, in the Charity Shield.

ODD DETAILS

⚽ Wilf McGuinness's playing career effectively ended when he broke his leg in a reserve game against Stoke City in December 1959. In 1966 he was named as substitute for an away game at Leicester City, but didn't play.

⚽ Ian Ure is thought to have had the shortest-ever name in League soccer, though strictly speaking his first name was John.

⚽ United players Harry Stafford, Harold Hardman, Les Olive and Bobby Charlton all went on to become club directors.

⚽ Defender Arnold Sidebottom, who played fifteen times for United in 1972–73 and 1973–74, was also a cricketer with Yorkshire and later played in one test match for England.

⚽ Freddie Goodwin, a United player from 1954 to 1960, appeared eleven times for Lancashire Cricket Club.

⚽ Ian Donald, a United full-back in the early 1970s, later became chairman of Aberdeen.

⚽ Warren Bradley won two FA Amateur Cup medals with Bishop Auckland in 1956 and 1957.

⚽ Sean Connery was offered a trial at Old Trafford in the 1950s, but instead chose to pursue stardom as an actor.

6 RED RESULTS

VICTORIES

⚽ United's best win and best home win was 10–0, against Anderlecht in the European Cup on 26 September 1956 at Maine Road.

⚽ United's best home League wins are:

10–1	v. Wolves (d 1)	15 October 1892
9–0	v. Walsall Town Swifts (d2)	3 April 1895
9–0	v. Darwen (d2)	24 December 1898
At Old Trafford		
9–0	v. Ipswich Town (pr)	4 March 1995

⚽ The 10–1 win over Wolves was United's first-ever League victory in only their seventh League game. It was also the first 10–1 scoreline in League football.

⚽ Walsall's 9–0 defeat might have been far worse. On 9 March 1895 United had beaten Walsall 14–0, which would still be the biggest win in League history. But Walsall protested about the state of the pitch, the result was nullified, and the fixture was replayed.

⚽ United's best away wins are:

7–0	v. Grimsby Town (d2)	26 December 1899
8–1	v. Nottingham Forest (pr)	6 February 1999

DEFEATS

⚽ United's worst defeat is 0–7, on three occasions:

0–7	v. Blackburn Rovers (d1) (a)	10 April 1926
0–7	v. Aston Villa (d1) (a)	27 December 1930
0–7	v. Wolves (d2) (a)	26 December 1931

⚽ The last two 0–7 defeats were Christmas holiday games, twelve months apart.

⚽ United's worst post-war defeats are:

0–6	v. Leicester City (d1) (a)	21 January 1961
0–6	v. Ipswich Town (d1) (a)	1 March 1980

⚽ United's worst home defeats are:

0–6	v. Aston Villa (d1)	14 March 1914
0–6	v. Huddersfield Town (d1)	10 September 1930
1–7	v. Newcastle United (d1)	10 September 1927
0–5	v. Manchester City (d1)	12 February 1955
2–7	v. Sheffield Wednesday (FAC)	1 February 1961
1–5	v. Bolton Wanderers (d2) (worst in d2)	9 September 1933

⚽ The Sheffield Wednesday loss came only eleven days after United's worst post-war away defeat at Leicester City.

⚽ The worst recent home defeats:

0–4	v. Notts. Forest	17 Dec. 1977 (last 4-goal margin)
0–3	v. York (LC)	20 Sept 1995
1–4	v. QPR	1 Jan. 1992 (last 4 against)
3–5	v. WBA	30 Dec. 1978 (last 5 against)

MOST VICTORIES

⚽ United won 28 League matches in 1905–06 (division two) and in 1956–57 (division one).

⚽ The most United wins in a season in all competitions was 41 in 1993–94: 27 in the League, 6 in the League Cup, 6 in the FA Cup and two in the European Cup. The record number of wins by any team in a season is 43, by Everton in 1984–85.

⚽ United also achieved 39 domestic wins in 1993–94, which is almost certainly an all-time English record. Spurs won 37 domestic matches in their 1960–61 Double season.

⚽ United's most away wins in a season in all competitions was 22, in 1993–94 – 20 on opponents' grounds and 2 on neutral venues. This is probably an all-time English record.

FEWEST LEAGUE VICTORIES

⚽ United (as Newton Heath) won only 6 games out of 30 in each of their first two seasons, 1892–93 and 1893–94.

⚽ United won only 7 games out of 42 in 1930–31. The club's post-war record low is 10 out of 42, in 1973–74.

⚽ The fewest home wins in a League season was 5 in 1893–94, which was only a 30-game season. The fewest home wins in a 42-game season was 6, in 1919–20, 1930–31 and 1962–63.

⚽ United did not win a single away match in 1892–93, the club's first season in League football. United achieved only a single away win in 1901–02 (division two), 1914–15, 1921–22, 1930–31 and 1986–87.

MOST LEAGUE DEFEATS

⚽ United's most defeats in a season was 27, from 42 games, in 1930–31.

⚽ Post-war, the most defeats in a season was 20, in 1973–74.

⚽ The most home defeats in a season was 9, in both 1930–31 and 1962–63.

⚽ The most away defeats in a season was 18, in 1930–31.

⚽ Post-war, the most away defeats in a season was 13, in both 1960–61 and 1973–74.

FEWEST DEFEATS

⚽ The fewest League defeats recorded by United in any season is three, during the 1998–99 campaign. The League record for fewest defeats is held by Arsenal, who lost just one match during the 1990–91 season.

⚽ United's fewest defeats in all competitions in any season was also during 1998–99. United lost five times in all – on three occasions in the League, once in the League Cup and once in the Charity Shield.

DRAWS

⚽ United drew 18 games out of 42 in 1980–81, 11 of them at home.

⚽ The most 0–0 draws in a season was 7, in 1972–73.

⚽ The side recorded 3 successive 0–0 draws in September 1921.

⚽ The lowest number of draws in a United season was 2, out of 30 games in 1893–94; and from 42 matches in 1934–35. The lowest number in a post-war season was 7, in 1959–60, 1963–64 and 1995–96.

⚽ United's longest sequence of draws in League and cup was 6, between 16 September and 3 October 1992.

⚽ The longest sequence of League draws was also 6, between 30 October and 27 November 1988, but this was interrupted by a League Cup defeat.

⚽ The most successive home League draws is five, between 8 November and 26 December 1980.

⚽ Eight successive away draws were recorded between 21 January and 22 April 1967, in the run-in to the 1966–67 championship win. And yet United recorded no other away draws all season.

⚽ United drew 4 successive League games by the same score, 1–1, between 2 September and 23 September 1978.

⚽ United drew their last 4 League matches of the 1926–27 season.

WINNING SEQUENCES

⚽ United won 14 consecutive League games from 15 October 1904 to 3 January 1905 in division two. This is an all-time League record, though it was later emulated by Bristol City and Preston North End, also in second division seasons. Strangely, United failed to win promotion in 1905.

⚽ United's best start to a League season is 10 wins, from 17 August 1985 to 28 September 1985. They then drew 1–1 at Luton Town on 5 October, thus falling one short of Tottenham Hotspur's record of 11 successive opening wins in 1960–61.

⚽ The start of the 1985–86 season also saw United's longest run of wins in the top division equalled. They had previously achieved 10 successive wins in division one between 21 September and 23 November 1907. The most consecutive wins ever recorded in the top flight was 13, by Spurs in 1960.

⚽ United are one of only five clubs to have won 10 consecutive League games on three occasions – in 1904–05, 1907 and 1985.

⚽ United won 16 successive competitive home games between 6 January 1951 and 8 September 1951.

⚽ United had 18 successive home League wins in division two between 15 October 1904 and 23 September 1905.

⚽ Both in the top division and post-war, United's best run of home League wins was 13, between 13 January and 8 September 1951.

⚽ United's best finish to a season has been 7 successive victories, achieved twice – in 1980–81, when manager Dave Sexton was subsequently sacked, and in 1992–93, when they won the League.

⚽ United's longest run of away League victories is 7, between 5 April and 28 August 1993 – at Norwich City, Coventry City, Crystal Palace and Wimbledon at the end of the 1992–93 season, and then Norwich (again), Aston Villa and Southampton at the start of 1993–94. This run was interrupted by the 1993 Charity Shield which ended in a draw, though United won on penalties. In 1960 Tottenham Hotspur had recorded 10 consecutive away League wins.

⚽ United's longest sequence of away wins in all competitions is six, recorded on four occasions, between:

---

20 August and 24 September 1985

9 January and 20 February 1994

16 January and 4 March 1996

16 January and 13 March 1999

⚽ The best sequence of League wins without conceding a goal is seven, in division two between 15 October and 3 December 1904. In the top division United had five wins without conceding a goal between 24 August and 12 September 1992.

UNBEATEN SEQUENCES

⚽ United's best undefeated run in League and cup is 34 games, between 25 September 1993 and 2 March 1994.

⚽ After losing at home to Middlesbrough on 19 December 1998, United established a run of 33 games unbeaten which extended up until victory in the 1999 European Cup final but was broken by the 2–1 defeat by Arsenal in the Charity Shield on 1 August 1999 (though some people don't regard this as a proper competitive match). The English record is 40 games undefeated, set by Nottingham Forest in 1978.

⚽ United's best undefeated League run is 26 games, from 4 February to 13 October 1956.

⚽ An undefeated League run from the start of the season of 15 matches was achieved from 17 August to 2 November 1985. United lost 1–0 at Sheffield Wednesday on 9 November.

UNBEATEN AT HOME

⚽ United have been unbeaten at home in all competitions in only three seasons: over 22 games in 1896–97, 21 games in 1955–56 and 29 games in 1982–83.

⚽ The side remained undefeated at home in the League in six seasons: 1894–95, 1896–97, 1955–56, 1966–67, 1982–83 and 1995–96. In 1966–67 and 1995–96 their unbeaten runs were spoilt only by losing to lower division sides in cup competitions.

⚽ United's longest undefeated home League run is 37 games, between 27 April 1966 and 20 January 1968.

⚽ The longest undefeated home run in all competitions is 36 games, achieved between 21 November 1992 and 13 February 1994. This falls well short of Liverpool's run of 86 home games unbeaten between 1978 and 1981.

UNBEATEN AWAY

⚽ United's longest undefeated run in League and cup away from home is 20 games, achieved on two occasions, between 2 October 1993 and 22 March 1994, and between 5 December 1998 and 26 May 1999.

⚽ The longest run of away League matches unbeaten is 14, between 11 February and 27 October 1956. After losing 3–1 at Sheffield Wednesday on 21 November 1998 United established a run of 13 away League games unbeaten which remains unbroken at the time of writing.

SEQUENCES WITHOUT A WIN

⚽ The worst sequence without a League win was 16 games – the last 14 of them defeats – between 19 April and 25 October 1930, a period of more than six months. There was a similar run of 16 League games without a win between 3 November 1928 and 9 February 1929, but this was interrupted by a home victory in the FA Cup.

⚽ The same period saw the worst United run without a home League win: 9 games between 3 November 1928 and 2 February 1929, interrupted by the same cup victory.

⚽ United went 26 away League games without a win, and 29 away games in League and cup, from 15 February 1930 to 3 April 1931.

⚽ United's worst post-war sequences without a League win were both of 11 games, from 11 December 1971 to 8 March 1972, and from 25 November 1989 to 3 February 1990, though both sequences were interrupted by FA Cup victories.

⚽ The worst post-war run without a win in any competition was 10 games between 30 September and 2 December 1961.

⚽ United's worst post-war run without a home League win was 7 games, between 22 February and 23 April 1958, just after Munich, though this was interrupted by home cup wins; and also between 8 February and 29 March 1978.

⚽ The longest post-war run without any home win was 8 matches, between 28 January and 29 March 1978.

SEQUENCES OF DEFEATS

⚽ United lost their first 12 League matches in 1930–31 before picking up their first points in a win over Birmingham City on 1 November. This is the longest-ever run of defeats from the start of the season by any club in the top division.

⚽ United lost 14 successive League games between 26 April and 25 October 1930.

⚽ These atrocious runs include the worst sequence of three defeats in United history, in September 1930, when United lost 6–2 at Chelsea, 6–0 at home to Huddersfield Town and 7–4 at home to Newcastle United. In these last two games, thirteen goals were conceded at home in just four days. The next two matches were ordinary 3–0 defeats.

⚽ The worst run of consecutive home defeats is 6, between 3 May 1930 and 18 October 1930.

⚽ The worst post-war run of home defeats is 3, which has occurred four times – between 2 and 26 December 1950, between 30 September and 28 October 1961, between 8 January and 12 February 1972 (though this was interrupted by an FA Cup win) and between 26 December 1978 and 3 February 1979.

⚽ United lost 17 away League games in a row between 26 April 1930 and 21 February 1931.

⚽ United's longest run of away defeats in all competitions is 15, between 30 September 1893 and 8 September 1894 (as Newton Heath). The side lost 14 away games out of 15 in the 1893–94 season, and between 3 December 1892 and 8 September 1894 lost 25 away games out of 26.

⚽ The worst finish to a season was also 1893–94, when they lost their last 4 League games.

ODD REVERSALS

⚽ On 31 December 1892, Newton Heath beat Derby County 7–1 at home. In the next match, at Stoke City, they lost 7–1.

⚽ In the 1897–98 season Newton Heath beat Woolwich Arsenal 5–1 at home, having lost 5–1 to them in London seven weeks before.

⚽ In 1928–29 United beat Newcastle United 5–0 at Old Trafford, but lost 5–0 at St James' Park.

⚽ On Christmas Day 1931, United beat Wolverhampton Wanderers 3–2 at home, only to lose 7–0 at Molineux on Boxing Day, one of United's three all-time worst defeats.

⚽ In 1960–61 Everton beat United 4–0 at Goodison Park, and United beat them by the same score at Old Trafford.

⚽ On Boxing Day 1963, United lost 6–1 away to Burnley. Two days later they beat them 5–1 at Old Trafford.

⚽ On 16 October 1965, United lost 5–1 away to Tottenham Hotspur, but nine weeks later, on 18 December, they beat Spurs 5–1 at Old Trafford.

REPEAT RESULTS

⚽ In 1898–99 United beat Luton Town 5–0 at home and 1–0 away. The following season, exactly the same scores were recorded.

⚽ In 1949–50 United beat Huddersfield Town 6–0 at home, and won by the exact same score at home the following season.

⚽ In 1961–62 United drew 2–2 at home with Leicester City and lost 4–3 away. Precisely the same results occurred the following year.

RESULTS AGAINST PARTICULAR CLUBS

⚽ United drew the only two League games they ever played against Accrington Stanley.

⚽ Between 1971 and 1978 United conceded 3 goals on each of seven successive visits to Arsenal – six in the League and one in the League Cup.

⚽ In 1949–50, over two League games, United built up an 11–0 aggregate score against Aston Villa, winning 7–0 at home and 4–0 away.

⚽ In 1980–81 United drew both League games with Aston Villa 3–3.

⚽ United won 6–5 at Chelsea in 1954–55, the season the London club were League champions.

⚽ Since 1966 United have beaten Chelsea only twice in the League at Old Trafford, and yet they have won 12 times at Stamford Bridge in the same period. Among United's regular League opponents, Chelsea is the most fruitful away venue by far, with wins in 28 of the 57 visits since 1905. In contrast, United have beaten Chelsea only 22 times at home. Between 1966 and 1986 United failed to beat Chelsea in 13 League visits to Old Trafford, the worst home sequence against any club.

⚽ Chelsea have conceded 106 League goals at home to United, and are the only club to have let in a century of League goals to the Reds on their own ground.

⚽ On 3 November 1973 Chelsea were winning 2–0 at Old Trafford with two minutes to go, but United then scored twice to end the match 2–2.

⚽ Chesterfield have lost on all ten League visits to United.

⚽ Doncaster Rovers have visited Old Trafford four times for League matches, but have yet to score there. Of the seventy-nine different clubs who have visited United for League fixtures, only Doncaster and Bristol Rovers have never scored.

◉ United were winning 4–1 with 26 minutes left at Derby County on 5 September 1936, but ended up losing 5–4.

◉ It is now more than eight years (at the time of publication, summer 1999) since United lost a League match after scoring the first goal. The last occasion was at Chelsea on 9 March 1991 when United eventually lost 3–2. Before losing their 1–0 lead over Arsenal in the August 1999 Charity Shield, the last time United lost any competitive match after scoring the first goal was in the FA Cup fifth round at Sheffield United on 14 February 1993.

◉ In between losing 3–2 at Sheffield Wednesday on 26 October 1991 and losing 3–2 at Coventry City on 28 December 1997, United went for more than six years without losing a League match after taking the lead.

RARE LEAGUE MEETINGS

◉ Nine teams have lost every League match they have played at United: Bristol Rovers (1 game), Chesterfield (10), Crewe Alexandra (2), Loughborough Town (5), Northampton Town (1), Oxford United (4), Rotherham United (3), Swindon Town (1) and York City (1).

◉ United's only perfect League records are against Crewe Alexandra, having won all four games, and York City, winning on the only two occasions they met in League competition.

◉ Six League sides have never drawn a League match against United: Crewe Alexandra, Leeds City, Nelson, New Brighton Town, Oxford United and York City.

◉ United lost 1–0 at home to all three newly promoted clubs in 1986–87 – Charlton Athletic, Norwich City and Wimbledon – and also failed to score against them away.

LEAGUE RECORD

⚽ Bolton Wanderers are the only current League team who have beaten United more often in the League than the Reds have beaten them. Bolton have 38 wins to United's 36. Two other clubs who are no longer in the League also achieved this: Bradford Park Avenue (9 wins to 8) and Burton Wanderers (3 to 2).

7 UNITED GOALS

HIGHEST SCORERS

⚽ United's all-time highest scorer is Bobby Charlton, with 199 League goals and 249 goals in all competitions.

⚽ Thirteen players have scored a hundred goals or more for United, and ten have achieved a hundred or more League goals:

		Seasons	League	Cup	Total
1	Bobby Charlton	1956–73	199	50*	249
2	Denis Law	1962–73	171	66*	237
3	Jack Rowley	1937–55	182	29*	211
=4	Dennis Viollet	1953–61	159	20*	179
	George Best	1963–74	137	42*	179
6	Joe Spence	1919–33	158	10	168
7	Mark Hughes	1983–95	120	43*	163
8	Stan Pearson	1937–53	128	21	149
9	David Herd	1961–68	114	31*	145
10	Tommy Taylor	1953–58	112	19*	131
11	Brian McClair	1987–98	88	39*	127
=12	Joe Cassidy	1893–1900	90	10	100
	Sandy Turnbull	1907–14	90	10	100

* Includes Charity Shield and European Super Cup.

⚽ In the middle of 1972–73 United had six players who had each scored a century of League goals with their various clubs – George Best, Bobby Charlton, Wyn Davies, Denis Law, Ted MacDougall and Ian Storey-Moore. Yet between them they scored only 25 League goals for United that season.

⚽ The most League goals by a United player in one season was 32 by Dennis Viollet during 1959–60 – in only 36 matches.

⚽ The highest goal total from all competitions in a season was 46 by Denis Law in 1963–64: 30 goals in the League, 10 in the FA Cup and 6 in the European Cup Winners' Cup.

GOALSCORING AVERAGES

⚽ Of the players to have made more than ten appearances for United, only two have averaged more than 2 goals every 3 games – Charlie Sagar and Tommy Taylor. A further fourteen players, including Dwight Yorke, have an average of more than one goal every two matches:

		Seasons	Goals	Games	Average
1	Charlie Sagar	1905–07	24	33	0.727
2	Tommy Taylor	1953–58	131	191	0.686*
3	Ronnie Burke	1946–49	23	35	0.657*
4	Jack Allan	1904–06	22	36	0.611
5	Dennis Viollet	1953–61	179	293	0.611*
6	Denis Law	1962–73	237	404	0.587*
7	Alex Dawson	1957–61	54	93	0.581
8	Jimmy Turnbull	1907–10	45	78	0.577*
9	Joe Cassidy	1893–1900	100	174	0.575
10	Dwight Yorke	1998–99	29	51	0.569
11	Tom Homer	1909–11	14	25	0.560
12	Henry Boyd	1897–99	33	59	0.559
13	David Herd	1961–68	145	265	0.547*

14	Ernie Goldthorpe	1922–24	16	30	0.533
15	Billy Whelan	1955–58	52	98	0.531*
16	Bill Rawlings	1928–29	19	36	0.528

* Includes Charity Shield and World Club Championship

The pre-Munich squad had four players with career averages of more than 1 goal every 2 games: Tommy Taylor, Dennis Viollet, Alex Dawson and Billy Whelan.

MOST GOALS IN ONE MATCH

The most goals by a United player in one match is 6, achieved twice: by Harold Halse against Swindon Town in the Charity Shield on 25 September 1911, and by George Best at Northampton Town in the FA Cup on 7 February 1970.

The most goals in a League game by a United player is 5, by Andy Cole in a home match against Ipswich Town on 4 March 1995.

MOST GOALS IN A SEASON

The most League goals by the team in a season is 103, in both 1956–57 and 1958–59.

United scored 143 goals in all competitions in 1956–57, which is probably a record for an English League club in one campaign. The total was made up of 103 goals in the League, 15 in the FA Cup, 24 in the European Cup and 1 in the Charity Shield. United's next best tally was 128 goals in the 1998–99 season – 80 League, 31 European Cup, 12 FA Cup and 5 in the League Cup.

Four players have been United's top League goalscorer in five different seasons – Joe Spence, Jack Rowley, George Best and Mark Hughes. In addition, Joe Spence was joint top League scorer in two other seasons.

⚽ Joe Spence, Jack Rowley, Denis Law and Mark Hughes were each United's top scorer in all competitions in five different seasons.

⚽ George Best is the only player to have been United's top League scorer in five successive seasons – from 1967–68 to 1971–72.

⚽ The most League goals conceded in a season is 115, in 1930–31.

⚽ The fewest goals by United's top scorer in a season was 6, by Bobby Charlton in 1972–73 and Sammy McIlroy in 1973–74. In all competitions in 1973–74, McIlroy and Lou Macari were joint top scorers with 6 each.

FASTEST GOALS

⚽ Ryan Giggs scored after 15 seconds against Southampton in November 1995.

⚽ Two of the fastest goals against United – both in 13 seconds – were by George Edwards for Aston Villa in the FA Cup in January 1948, and Alan Ball for Arsenal in November 1975.

⚽ United were winning 5–0 after just 22 minutes against West Bromwich Albion on 20 August 1966, the opening day of the 1966–67 season. United eventually won 5–3.

PROLIFIC SCORERS

⚽ At the beginning of the 1951–52 season, Jack Rowley scored 14 goals in seven games, including three hat-tricks in 22 days.

⚽ The longest run of League games in which one player has always scored is eight, by Billy Whelan between 5 September and 20 October 1956, and he scored just a single goal in each match. This run was interrupted, however, by two European Cup games in which Whelan failed to score.

⚽ Six is the longest run of games in all competitions in which the same United player has always managed to score. This has been achieved on several occasions, most recently by Dwight Yorke between 10 January and 6 February 1999.

⚽ In 1926–27, Frank McPherson scored in each of the opening five League games.

⚽ Steve Bruce scored 19 goals in 1990–91, said to be an all-time record for a defender. This included 11 penalties. He was also United's joint leading League scorer with 13 goals.

⚽ Steve Bruce is thought to have scored more goals than any other defender in post-war League football, having claimed 81 League goals for his clubs.

⚽ The United player with the longest goalscoring span was Jack Rowley. Seventeen years and 39 days separated his first goal for United on 4 December 1937 and his last on 12 January 1955.

⚽ United have scored 6 goals in an away League game on eighteen occasions, more than any other club. The most recent instances were the 6–2 win at Leicester City on 16 January 1999 and the 8–1 victory at Nottingham Forest on 6 February 1999.

⚽ United's longest run of scoring in every League game is 27 matches, during 1958–59. This sequence also includes 22 consecutive League games in which United scored at least twice.

⚽ United players have been the leading scorer in the top division on only three occasions:

1959–60	Dennis Viollet	32 goals
1967–68	George Best	28 goals
	(joint with Ron Davies of Southampton)	

1998–99	Dwight Yorke	18 goals
	(joint with Michael Owen of Liverpool and Jimmy Floyd Hasselbaink of Leeds)	

INFREQUENT SCORERS

◉ In April 1930 Hugh McLenahan scored 6 goals over five successive matches. Yet, strangely, he scored only 12 goals in all in 116 games with United.

◉ Shay Brennan scored twice on his debut for United in the famous post-Munich FA Cup match against Sheffield Wednesday, but scored only 4 more goals in another 355 games for United.

MOST SCORERS

◉ The most United goalscorers in one season was eighteen, in both 1899–1900 and 1994–95.

◉ The most United scorers in one match was six – Bob Donaldson (3), Willie Stewart (3), Adam Carson, Alf Farman, James Hendry and Billy Hood – in the record 10–1 win over Wolverhampton Wanderers on 15 October 1892.

◉ The 1973–74 relegation season was United's worst-ever season for League goals, yet remarkably, players wearing every shirt from 1 to 12 scored in that campaign.

◉ On three occasions five different United players have scored ten goals or more in the same season:

1964–65:	Law (39), Herd (28), Connelly (20), Charlton (18) and Best (14)
1993–94:	Cantona (25), Hughes (22), Giggs (17), Sharpe (11) and Kanchelskis (10)
1998–99:	Yorke (29), Cole (24), Solskjaer (18), Scholes (11) and Giggs (10)

❁ During the 1992–93 championship season, United goalscorers wore every shirt from 2 to 11.

❁ Over three successive games in 1992–93 – against Coventry City, Bury (FAC) and Tottenham Hotspur (all at home) – nine different players scored for United. This also occurred in 1898–99 and 1985–86.

❁ During four successive games in December 1992 and January 1993, eleven different players scored for United: Ryan Giggs, Mark Hughes, Eric Cantona, Lee Sharpe and Denis Irwin (v. Coventry); Mike Phelan and Keith Gillespie (v. Bury); Brian McClair and Paul Parker (v. Spurs); Paul Ince and Andrei Kanchelskis (v. Queen's Park Rangers (a)).

STOUT DEFENCE

❁ The fewest League goals conceded by United in one season was 23 in 1924–25, which remains a record for the second division.

❁ United's best defensive record in the top division was 26 goals conceded, in the 1997–98 season.

❁ United's longest run of League games without conceding a goal is seven, achieved on three occasions:

---

15 Oct. to 3 Dec. 1904 (d2)

20 Sep. to 1 Nov. 1924 (d2)

8 May to 30 Aug. 1997 (pr)

❁ Between April and December 1994 United went a record 12 home League games without conceding a goal, a feat previously achieved by Notts County in 1972–73 and Cambridge United in 1982–83, but probably not exceeded by any side. United's run lasted 18 hours and 55 minutes.

❁ 1994–95 also saw the fewest home League goals scored against United in a season – just 4 – conceded over three games. Liverpool have also conceded only 4 home League goals in a season, in 1978–79, but theirs were given away over four games. So the side's 18 home clean sheets in 1994–95 probably constitutes an all-time League record for a 42-game campaign.

⚽ United's longest run of League games from the start of the season without conceding a goal is five, between 10 and 30 August 1997.

⚽ The most clean sheets in a season was 25 in the second division in 1924–25, when goalkeeper Alf Steward played in every game. The most clean sheets in the top division was 24 in 1993–94, and Peter Schmeichel kept goal for all but three of them.

⚽ United's best goal difference was 62 in 1905–06, when they scored 90 goals and conceded just 28. But this is 23 fewer than the all-time League record of 85 achieved by Bradford City in 1928–29.

⚽ The highest goal aggregate for a season was 182 in 1959–60, when United scored 102 goals and conceded 80.

⚽ The lowest goal aggregate for a season was 78 in 1980–81, when United scored only 42 goals and conceded 36.

⚽ United's best goal average was 2.807 in the 1997–98 season, when they scored 73 goals and conceded only 26.

GOAL DROUGHT

⚽ United have gone five League games without scoring on three occasions: 22 February to 17 March 1902 (division two), 26 January to 23 February 1924 (division two) and 7 February to 7 March 1981 (division one).

⚽ In League and cup, United went six games without a goal between 26 January and 23 February 1924.

⚽ United's fewest League goals in a season (since 1904–5, when the top two divisions were expanded to twenty clubs each) was 38 in 1973–74. This campaign also saw the most games in which United failed to score – nineteen.

✪ Since 1904–05, United's lowest away League goal total in one season was 14 in 1986–87.

✪ In twenty-three League appearances with United (including nine as substitute), forward Terry Gibson scored only once. Yet Gibson scored six times against United – three goals for Coventry City before he came to Old Trafford, and three for Wimbledon afterwards.

✪ After the England striker Garry Birtles joined United in 1980 he waited thirty League games before scoring his first League goal for the club, though he did manage to score once in the FA Cup.

✪ Of United's outfield players, Charlie Moore appeared most often without scoring. He played 328 times between 1919 and 1930.

OWN GOALS

✪ In October 1923, Sam Wynne of Oldham Athletic scored two goals for his side and two own goals for United. This has happened only twice in League history.

✪ Another to score two own goals for United was Murca of the Portuguese side Porto in November 1977 in the Cup-Winners' Cup at Old Trafford.

✪ Phil Beal of Spurs, with own goals in both December 1965 and August 1968, scored more often for United than Terry Gibson did.

✪ United have benefitted from six own goals by opponents in three different seasons: 1975–76, 1996–97 and 1997–98.

✪ Nobby Stiles had the misfortune to score two own goals for Manchester City – at Old Trafford on 23 September 1961, and at Maine Road on 21 January 1967. In the first game he also scored for United.

⚽ At Sheffield Wednesday in October 1987, Bryan Robson scored both for and against United.

GOALSCORING FEATS

⚽ In 1905–06 United began by winning 5–1, and finished the season with a 6–0 win. The team scored 5 goals or more in ten of the season's League and cup games. The start of 1906 saw 5 or more goals scored in eight matches out of fifteen, with the following sequence: 5–0, 7–2 (FAC), 0–3, 5–2, 1–0, 3–0 (FAC), 5–1, 0–0, 5–1 (FAC), 5–0, 2–3 (FAC), 4–1, 0–1, 5–2, 5–1.

⚽ United striker Ted MacDougall was the first player to be leading goalscorer in three separate divisions: with Bournemouth & Boscombe Athletic in the fourth (1970–71) and third (1971–72) divisions before he came to Old Trafford, and later with Norwich City (1975–76) in the first division.

⚽ In the 2–0 victory at Southampton in March 1990, Colin Gibson scored with his last kick of the game before being substituted, then Mark Robins scored with his first kick after coming on as a substitute (though not as a replacement for Gibson).

⚽ United have scored a record 40 goals in the FA Charity Shield.

⚽ When United beat Walsall Town Swifts 9–0 in April 1895, four players scored two goals each – Joe Cassidy, Bob Donaldson, James Peters and Dick Smith.

⚽ The above victory over Walsall also saw the most goals in one half, with United (Newton Heath) scoring 8 after the interval.

⚽ Denis Law scored against Gordon Banks at Wembley for three different sides: for United against Leicester City in the 1963 FA Cup final, for the Rest of the World against England in 1963, and for Scotland against England, in both 1965 and

1967.

⚽ Of Lee Sharpe's first 11 goals for United, 4 came in semi-finals: one in each leg of the 1991 League Cup semi-final, another in the 1991 European Cup-Winners' Cup semi-final, and one at home in the 1992 League Cup semi-final. Of Sharpe's first 5 goals at Old Trafford, 3 were in semi-finals.

⚽ Bryan Robson scored at least one League goal in each of the twenty-one seasons from 1974–75 to 1994–95, for either West Bromwich Albion, United or Middlesbrough.

⚽ In 1994–95 David Beckham scored in the European Cup with United, and also in the third division (the old fourth division) while on loan to Preston North End.

⚽ Ian Rush scored more than 300 goals for Liverpool in his career, but failed to score in his first twenty-four matches against United. He broke his duck in April 1992, during what was Rush's worst League season up to that point.

⚽ Lee Chapman scored against United for six different clubs in fourteen years: Stoke City (December 1980), Sunderland (February 1984), Sheffield Wednesday (April 1985), Nottingham Forest (March 1989), Leeds United (August 1991) and West Ham United (February 1994).

OLDEST SCORERS

⚽ United's oldest goalscorer was Billy Meredith at Derby County on 12 February 1921, at the age of 46 years and 201 days.

⚽ Bryan Robson became United's oldest post-war scorer when he hit the mark against Oldham Athletic in the 1994 FA Cup semi-final replay. The post-war scorers over thirty-five are:

Bryan Robson	Oldham (FAC SF replay) (n)	13 Apr. 1994	37 y, 92 d	
Jack Warner	Charlton (FAC) (h)	7 Feb. 1948	36 y, 139 d	79

Bill Foulkes	Real Madrid (ECC SF) (a)	15 May 1968	36 y, 131 d
Jimmy Delaney	Charlton (h)	16 Sept 1950	36 y, 13 d
Bobby Charlton	Southampton (a)	31 Mar. 1973	35 y, 171 d
Steve Bruce	Bolton (a)	25 Feb. 1996	35 y, 56 d

⚽ Two of the three goals by United's oldest post-war scorers have come in semi-final matches.

YOUNGEST SCORER

⚽ Norman Whiteside became United's youngest post-war scorer, against Stoke City on 15 May 1982, aged 17 years and 7 days. He is also most likely United's youngest-ever scorer.

DEBUT GOALS

⚽ Harold Halse scored after just 30 seconds on his debut for United against The Wednesday (now Sheffield Wednesday) on 28 March 1908. Peter Barnes scored after five minutes of his debut at Nottingham Forest on 31 August 1985.

⚽ When Ole Gunnar Solskjaer notched a goal against Blackburn Rovers on 25 August 1996 he became the first United substitute to score on his debut.

⚽ Alex Dawson scored on his debut in each of the three domestic competitions: against Burnley in the League in April 1957, Sheffield Wednesday in the FA Cup in February 1958, and Exeter City in the League Cup in October 1960.

⚽ Tommy Reid scored twice on his League debut for United against West Ham United in February 1929, and got a hat-trick on his FAC debut for the club at Stoke City two years later.

⚽ Only one player, Charlie Sagar, has scored a hat-trick on his debut for United – against Bristol City in September

1905 – but nine others have scored twice in their first match: William Brooks, Jack Allan, George Livingstone, George Nicol, Tommy Reid, Tommy Taylor, Bobby Charlton, Shay Brennan and Paul Scholes.

⚽ Neil Webb scored only 11 goals for United, but managed to hit the mark on his club debut in four different competitions – the League, the FA Cup, the League Cup and the European Cup-Winners' Cup.

⚽ David Herd scored in his first United game in each of five different cup competitions – the FA and League Cups, and the three main European trophies – but he failed to score on his League debut for the club.

8 RED HAT-TRICKS

MORE THAN A HAT-TRICK

⚽ When Andy Cole scored 5 against Ipswich Town in March 1995, it was the first time a United player had ever scored that many goals in a League match.

⚽ The only other occasions on which a United player has scored 5 or more are:

Harold Halse	6 v. Swindon Town (CS)	(n)	25 Sept. 1911
George Best	6 v. Northampton Town (FAC)	(a)	7 Feb. 1970
Jack Rowley	5 v. Yeovil Town (FAC)	(h)	12 Feb. 1949

⚽ Jack Rowley and Denis Law each scored 4 goals on four occasions, though one of Rowley's was a 5, which Law never achieved.

⚽ Dick Smith is the only United player to get 4 goals against Manchester City, and it was in the very first derby game, in November 1894.

⚽ Ole Gunnar Solskjaer scored four goals in the space of thirteen minutes when United beat Nottingham Forest 8-1 on 6 February 1999. This was the first hat-trick by a United substitute and is also thought to be the first time a substitute has scored four goals in any League game.

HAT-TRICKS GALORE

⚽ Jack Rowley scored three hat-tricks in the first seven games of the 1951–52 season.

⚽ Dennis Viollet scored hat-tricks against Burnley at home and away in 1960–61.

⚽ Henry Boyd got hat-tricks in the first two games of the season in 1897–98, against Lincoln City (h) and Burton Swifts (a).

⚽ Chris Taylor scored only 6 League goals for United in 28 appearances, and they all came in two hat-tricks at the end of the 1925–26 season.

DOUBLE HAT-TRICKS

⚽ During 1898–99 United players got only two League hat-tricks all season, but they were both scored in the same game: against Darwen on Christmas Eve 1898, by William Bryant and Joe Cassidy.

⚽ Two United players have scored hat-tricks in the same match on six occasions:

Bob Donaldson and Willie Stewart	v. Wolves (h)	15 Dec. 1892
Bob Donaldson and Alf Farman	v. Derby (h)	31 Dec. 1892
William Bryant and Joe Cassidy	v. Darwen (h)	24 Dec. 1898
Sandy Turnbull and Jimmy Turnbull	v. Blackburn (FAC) (h)	20 Feb. 1909
Dennis Viollet (4) and Tommy Taylor	v. Anderlecht (ECC) (h)	26 Sept. 1956
Dennis Viollet and Albert Quixall	v. Burnley (h)	12 Apr. 1961

MOST BY ONE PLAYER

⚽ The most United hat-tricks by one player was eighteen

by Denis Law, including a record seven during the 1963–64 season. He also got hat-tricks in all three European competitions.

 In 1968–69 Denis Law scored a hat-trick in each leg of the European Cup first-round tie with Waterford.

YOUNGEST HAT-TRICK

 United's youngest hat-trick scorer – and thought to be the youngest hat-trick scorer in League history – was Jack Rowley when he hit four against Swansea Town in December 1937. Rowley was 17 years and 58 days old, and it was only his second game for the club.

 United's youngest post-war hat-trick was by Alex Dawson against Fulham in the 1958 FA Cup semi-final replay, at the age of 18 years and 33 days.

 United's youngest post-war League hat-trick was by Andy Ritchie, against Leeds in March 1979, at the age of 18 years and 118 days.

FASTEST HAT-TRICK

 It may never be resolved which United player has scored the quickest hat-trick for the club. In February 1923 Ernie Goldthorpe scored three times between the 62nd and 66th minutes of United's match at Notts County. On the opposite bank of the Trent, Ole Gunnar Solskjaer scored three times in the last five minutes of United's match against Nottingham Forest on 6 February 1999.

HAT-TRICK VICTIMS

 When Dwight Yorke scored three goals at Filbert Street in the Reds' 6–2 win on 16 January 1999 it was the sixth time a United player has scored a hat-trick at Leicester City.

⚽ Between 1954 and 1960 United players scored hat-tricks at Burnley on three occasions.

⚽ Denis Law scored hat-tricks at Ipswich Town two seasons running, in 1962–63 and 1963–64.

⚽ In November 1966 David Herd's hat-trick against Sunderland was scored past three different goalkeepers: Jim Montgomery, who went off injured, then his first stand-in, Charlie Hurley, and finally John Parke.

⚽ Newcastle United conceded a hat-trick in visits to Old Trafford in both the League Cup and the League during the 1976–77 season.

HAT-TRICK DROUGHTS

⚽ The 1972–73 season was the first post-war campaign in which no United player got a hat-trick.

⚽ After Mark Hughes scored a League Cup hat-trick against Southampton in January 1991, United went 214 games without another, until Andrei Kanchelskis got three against Manchester City in November 1994. Ironically, this gap of almost four years was one of the most successful periods in United history, and the club took five major trophies.

⚽ After Mark Hughes scored three against Millwall in September 1989, United went a club record 209 games without a League hat-trick, until Andrei Kanchelskis got three against Manchester City in November 1994. During this period United won the championship twice and were also runners-up.

⚽ For more than twenty-one years, between August 1977 and January 1999, no United player scored a hat-trick away from home in the League. Then two were grabbed within three weeks – by Dwight Yorke at Leicester City on 16 January and Ole Gunnar Solskjaer at Forest on 6 February 1999.

ODD HAT-TRICKS

⚽ In 1930–31 United scored only two League hat-tricks – and were beaten both times. Tommy Reid got three as United lost 7–4 at home to Newcastle United, and Jimmy Bullock scored three at Leicester City where United went down 5–4.

⚽ Charlie Mitten's four goals against Aston Villa in March 1950 – including a hat-trick of penalties – were the last he ever scored for United. In June 1950 Mitten left England to play soccer in Colombia.

⚽ Bobby Charlton notched up his first hat-trick in February 1957, suitably enough at Charlton Athletic.

⚽ Andy Ritchie twice scored a hat-trick and then was dropped. After getting three against Leeds United in March 1979, he was only substitute for the following game and was not brought on. A year later he scored three against Tottenham Hotspur, and survived only one more game in the team.

⚽ Bryan Robson's only hat-trick during his thirteen years with United came while playing for England in Turkey in November 1984.

⚽ Paul Scholes also scored three goals for England against Poland in March 1999 but has yet to achieve a hat-trick for United.

HAT-TRICKS CONCEDED

⚽ In October 1927, Dixie Dean scored five goals for Everton against United.

⚽ The last hat-trick conceded at Old Trafford was scored by Dennis Bailey of Queen's Park Rangers when they beat United 4–1 on New Year's Day 1992. Subsequently Bailey scored only one more league goal for QPR.

⚽ United have suffered the indignity of conceding four

goals to a single visiting player at Old Trafford on at least three occasions:

George Camsell of Middlesbrough	2 May 1931
Ron Davies of Southampton	16 August 1969
Martin Peters of Tottenham Hotspur	28 October 1972

9 UNITED GOALKEEPERS

STAND-IN KEEPERS

☉ At Stoke City in January 1893, United (then Newton Heath) played with only ten men and used three different goalkeepers after the regular keeper, Jimmy Warner, missed the train. Three outfield players – Willie Stewart, Tommy Fitzsimmons and John Clements – took it in turns to keep goal. Not surprisingly, United lost 7–1.

☉ Half-back Walter Cartwright played in goal on two occasions, at Rotherham in March 1896 and at Doncaster in February 1903.

☉ In February 1901 goalkeeper Jimmy Whitehouse played at Walsall in the inside-left position.

☉ Johnny Carey's single appearance in goal was at Sunderland in February 1953, when he was called upon in an emergency to play the whole game.

☉ On 8 May 1956 Jackie Blanchflower played in goal for the whole of a friendly match against Helsingborg.

☉ Other United stand-in goalkeepers in post-war years have included:

Duncan Edwards for Ray Wood	Man. City (CS) (a)	Oct. 1956
Jackie Blanchflower for Ray Wood	Aston Villa (FAC final) (W)	May 1957
Alex Dawson for Harry Gregg	Spurs (h)	Jan. 1961
David Herd for Harry Gregg	Liverpool (h)	Nov. 1963
David Herd for Harry Gregg	Blackburn (h)	Nov. 1965
David Sadler for Alex Stepney	Arsenal (a)	Aug. 1970
Brian Greenhoff for Alex Stepney	Birmingham (a)	Aug. 1975

UNFORTUNATE KEEPERS

⚽ When Irish international goalkeeper Tommy Breen made his debut against Leeds United in November 1936, he conceded a goal after just 60 seconds, before he had even touched the ball.

⚽ In January 1938, in an FA Cup tie at Barnsley, Tommy Breen touched a long throw-in into his own goal, resulting in the only recorded instance of a goal scored directly from a throw-in.

⚽ Ronnie Briggs conceded 14 goals in his first three games for United in 1961. They lost 6–0 at Leicester City in the League, drew 1–1 at Sheffield Wednesday in the FA Cup, and lost the replay at home 7–2.

⚽ On 30 December 1978, Gary Bailey conceded two goals to Tony Brown in a 5–3 defeat by West Bromwich Albion. Fifteen years before, in September 1963, his father, Roy Bailey, had conceded a goal to Brown while keeping goal for Ipswich.

OUTSTANDING KEEPERS

⚽ Pat Dunne was not on the losing side in his first 19 games in goal for United in 1964.

⚽ Jimmy Rimmer helped two clubs win the League and then the European Cup: United in 1967 and 1968, and Aston Villa in 1981 and 1982 – fourteen years later.

⚽ United lost 6–0 at Ipswich in March 1980, but Gary Bailey prevented a record defeat by saving two penalties. It could be argued that he made three saves, as one penalty had to be retaken.

⚽ In just 56 games with United, Les Sealey claimed an extraordinary haul of cup honours: an FA Cup medal (1990), a European Cup-Winners' Cup medal (1991) and two League Cup finalists' medals (1991 and 1994).

⚽ At 6 feet 4 inches (1.93 m), Peter Schmeichel is thought to have been United's tallest-ever goalkeeper.

⚽ Peter Schmeichel had the most successful start of any United goalkeeper, with four clean sheets in August 1991. The next best is two clean sheets.

⚽ Schmeichel boasts the longest League run for a keeper at United: 94 games, between 14 March 1992 and 1 May 1994.

⚽ In 1994–95 Peter Schmeichel let in only one League goal at Old Trafford all season, against Southampton, in the very last of his seventeen home League matches. Between April 1994 and May 1995 Schmeichel had also played seventeen home League games without letting in a goal – a total of 25 hours and 55 minutes – which is almost certainly a League record.

⚽ Peter Schmeichel boasts the most clean-sheets of any goalkeeper in United history – 179, compared with 175 for Alex Stepney, 161 for Gary Bailey and 98 for Alf Steward.

MOST GOALKEEPERS

⚽ During the spring and summer of 1991, United played four different goalkeepers in consecutive matches:

Gary Walsh	11 May	Crystal Palace (a)
Les Sealey	15 May	Barcelona (ECWC Final) (n)
Mark Bosnich	20 May	Tottenham Hotspur (h)
Peter Schmeichel	17 August	Notts County (h)

⚽ United had used four goalkeepers in four games on three previous occasions:

8 Feb.–14 Mar. 1896	Ridgway, Perrins, Cartwright and Whittaker
24 Feb.–17 Mar. 1934	Hall, Behan, Hillam and Hacking
7–17 Sept. 1966	Gregg, Gaskell, P.Dunne and Stepney

In the September 1966 case Harry Gregg, David Gaskell and Pat Dunne each played their last games for United in the space of just eight days, after substantial and distinguished careers for the club.

The most goalkeepers fielded by United in a season is five, during 1952–53: Ray Wood, Jack Crompton, Reg Allen, Johnny Carey and Les Olive.

United also fielded five goalkeepers during the 1991 calendar year – Les Sealey, Gary Walsh, Mark Bosnich, Peter Schmeichel and Ian Wilkinson – but the Scottish international Jim Leighton, who was also on United's books, didn't get a game all year.

BRIEF KEEPERS

One of the five keepers used in 1952–53, Les Olive, was an amateur who worked in the United ticket office; he later became club secretary, and then a director.

Mike Pinner, a former Cambridge blue who played four times in goal during 1960–61, was the last amateur to appear in the United first team.

Three goalkeepers played only one game for United: Billy Behan against Bury in March 1934, Tony Hawksworth against Blackpool in October 1956, and Ian Wilkinson against Cambridge United in the League Cup in 1991.

OLDEST KEEPERS

United's oldest goalkeeper, Jack Hacking, was 37 years and 42 days old when he played at Norwich City on 2 February 1935.

The club's oldest post-war keeper was Les Sealey, who appeared against Aston Villa in the League Cup final on 27 March 1994 aged 36 years and 179 days. Raimond van der

Gouw will take this record if he plays for United after 20 September 1999.

YOUNGEST KEEPER

⚽ United's youngest goalkeeper – and probably youngest ever player – was David Gaskell in the Charity Shield against Manchester City on 24 October 1956 at the age of 16 years and 19 days. Gaskell was probably also United's youngest League keeper just over a year later on 30 November 1957, when he played against Tottenham Hotspur aged 17 years and 56 days. It was not a happy League debut – he conceded a first-half hat-trick to Bobby Smith.

GOALSCORING KEEPERS

⚽ At the start of the 1973–74 season, Alex Stepney volunteered to take penalties. Having scored from the spot in a pre-season friendly shoot-out against the Uruguayan side Penarol, he got two in the League, against Leicester City and Birmingham City, but then missed against Wolverhampton Wanderers. From 20 October to 29 December he was United's joint top scorer. Only one other League goalkeeper since the war, Arthur Wilkie of Reading in 1962–63, has scored twice in a League season, and that was when he returned to the field from injury as an outfield player. So Stepney can claim to be one of the two highest-scoring goalkeepers in a season since the war.

⚽ Harry Gregg scored a penalty for United in a 10–1 friendly win against a Ukrainian National XI in Philadelphia in June 1960.

⚽ When Alex Dawson replaced the injured Harry Gregg in goal against Tottenham Hotspur in January 1961, Gregg took Dawson's place in the forward line and passed the ball for the second goal, scored by Mark Pearson.

⚽ In the Charity Shield in August 1967, United conceded a goal which Tottenham Hotspur goalkeeper Pat Jennings kicked the whole length of the pitch and over Alex Stepney's head.

⚽ Peter Schmeichel headed United's equalizing goal against Rotor Volgograd in the UEFA Cup in September 1995, and thus helped preserve the club's unbeaten home record in Europe – though it wasn't enough to win the tie. Schmeichel often ventured into the opposing penalty area for corners late in the game if United desperately needed a goal. Arguably, it was Schmeichel's presence in the Bayern Munich goal-mouth during a corner in the first minute of injury time during the 1999 European Cup final which led to Teddy Sheringham's equalising goal, and paved the way to victory less than two minutes later.

GOALKEEPERS' CAPS

⚽ Jimmy Rimmer and Phil Hughes both won international caps after leaving United. Rimmer later played for England while with Arsenal. Hughes only reached the United reserves, but subsequently played for Northern Ireland while with Bury.

⚽ In 1990–91 United had two international goalkeepers – Jim Leighton (Scotland) and Mark Bosnich (Australia) – and an England under-21 goalkeeper – Gary Walsh – but they played only one, two and six games respectively. Les Sealey, who kept all three internationals out of the side, never played for England at any level.

⚽ For a brief period in the close season of 1991, United had three full international goalkeepers on their books: Jim Leighton (Scotland), Mark Bosnich (Australia) and Peter Schmeichel (Denmark). In addition, Gary Walsh had won under-21 caps for England.

United have also fielded international goalkeepers from three other countries: Northern Ireland (e.g. Harry Gregg), England (e.g. Alex Stepney) and the Republic of Ireland (e.g. Pat Dunne).

John Sutcliffe, who played in goal for United in 1903–4, was a double soccer and rugby union international.

10 RED PENALTIES

MOST PENALTIES

⚽ Charlie Mitten scored a hat-trick of penalties against Aston Villa in March 1950, and also got one other goal. United went fifty-five games before scoring another penalty.

⚽ The most United penalties scored in a post-war season was 12, in 1990–91.

⚽ In August 1974 Gerry Daly scored 4 penalties in three games.

PENALTY DECIDERS

⚽ United were involved in the first penalty tie-breaker in England in August 1970 when they drew 1–1 in the Watney Cup semi-final at Hull City, and then won 4–3 on penalties.

⚽ In February 1992, United became the first top-division team to be eliminated from the FA Cup on penalties when they drew a fourth-round replay 1–1 at home to Southampton, and then lost 4–2 from the penalty spot.

NOTABLE PENALTIES

⚽ Arnold Muhren's first penalty for United was in the 1983 FA Cup final replay against Brighton & Hove Albion.

⚽ In 1994 Eric Cantona became the first player to score 2 penalties in an FA Cup final.

⚽ Eric Cantona scored another penalty against Blackburn Rovers in the Charity Shield the following August, making it

3 penalties in two successive Wembley visits.

PENALTY DROUGHTS

⚽ United went almost two years and 73 games without scoring a League penalty, between May 1988 and April 1990.

⚽ United did not score a single League penalty in 1988–89.

MOST RELIABLE PENALTY-TAKERS

⚽ Eric Cantona scored 18 penalties and only missed twice during competitive matches during his five years at Old Trafford. Remarkably, on only two occasions did the opposing goalkeeper dive the correct way.

⚽ Eric Cantona equals Albert Quixall in having scored the most post-war penalties for United – eighteen each. Quixall had four misses. Steve Bruce scored seventeen times from the spot and missed five times.

⚽ Proportionately, the most accurate of United's leading post-war penalty-takers was Gerry Daly with seventeen successes for United and just one miss during the mid-1970s. Steve Coppell has the best 100% record having scored three out of three taken.

⚽ It is said that Charlie Mitten scored eighteen consecutive penalties in his career, but the records suggest otherwise and show he missed four times during the 1948–49 and 1949–50 seasons. Mitten scored 16 penalties in competitive matches for United.

⚽ The most penalties scored in one season by a United player was 11, by Steve Bruce in 1990–91.

MISSED PENALTIES

⚽ United missed 6 penalties in 1984–85, but scored 11 others.

◉ The goalkeeper John Lukic has saved penalties from three different United players. While playing for Leeds United he saved Ashley Grimes's penalty in December 1979. Then, playing for Arsenal at Old Trafford, he saved from Norman Whiteside in December 1985 and from Brian McClair in August 1989. In addition, McClair blasted another penalty over Lukic's bar at Highbury in the FA Cup in February 1988.

◉ Four of United's current players have missed each of the penalties they have ever taken for the club:

Nicky Butt	v. Port Vale (LC)(h)	5 October 1994
Paul Scholes	v. Leicester City (LC)(a)	27 November 1996
Teddy Sheringham	v. Tottenham Hotspur (a)	10 August 1997
	v. Derby County (a)	18 October 1997
	v. Aston Villa (h)	15 December 1997
Dwight Yorke	v. Arsenal (h)	17 February 1999

◉ At the end of the home match against Aston Villa on 1 May 1999, United had five players on the pitch who had missed their last penalty for the club – Butt, Scholes, Sheringham and Yorke (see above), and Denis Irwin, who missed a penalty that day.

◉ Six other post-war players have missed the single penalties they took for United – Harry McShane, Tommy Taylor, Dennis Viollet, Brian Greenhoff, Gordon McQueen and John Gidman.

◉ When United lost 6-0 to Ipswich Town on 1 March 1980, the score might have been much worse had not Gary Bailey saved two penalties from Kevin Beattie and Frans Thijssen. Arguably Bailey made three saves since one of the missed penalties was retaken after Bailey saved it but he was deemed to have moved too early.

◉ Probably the most important penalty save in United history came in the final minute of normal time of the FA Cup semi-final replay against Arsenal on 14 April 1999 when Peter Schmeichel saved a penalty from Dennis Bergkamp. United went on to win the match 2–1, to take the FA Cup and, of course, secure the Treble.

⚽ At the time of writing (July 1999), United have not conceded a League penalty at Old Trafford since Norwich City on 4 December 1993. (During the same period opponents scored four penalties at Old Trafford in cup matches.)

11 RED CAPS

⚽ At the end of July 1999 United had nineteen full internationals on the books, one 'B' international, one under-23 international and four under-21 internationals:

Australia	Mark Bosnich
England	David Beckham, Wes Brown, Nicky Butt, Andy Cole, Gary Neville, Phil Neville, Paul Scholes and Teddy Sheringham
Netherlands	Jordi Cruyff, Jaap Stam
Norway	Henning Berg, Ronny Johnsen, Ole Gunnar Solskjaer
Republic of Ireland	Denis Irwin, Roy Keane
Sweden	Jesper Blomqvist
Trindad and Tobago	Dwight Yorke
Wales	Ryan Giggs
'B' International	
England	John Curtis
Under-23 International	
Norway	Erik Nevland
Under-21 Internationals	
England	Michael Clegg, Jonathan Greening
Northern Ireland	David Healy
Scotland	Alex Notman

MOST INTERNATIONAL CAPS

⚽ Bobby Charlton's total of 106 caps for England was a

record until 1973, when he was overtaken by Bobby Moore. Charlton is now in third place behind Peter Shilton on 125 and Moore on 108. Bryan Robson is fifth with 90 caps.

⚽ Denis Law was Scotland's most capped player from May 1974 until his record of 55 appearances was overtaken by Kenny Dalglish in June 1978.

⚽ Although Pat Jennings is Northern Ireland's most capped player with 119 appearances, the country's most capped outfield players all played for United – Mal Donaghy (91), Sammy McIlroy (88), Jimmy Nicholl (73) and David McCreery (67).

⚽ Paul McGrath is the Republic of Ireland's most capped player, with 83 appearances.

INTERNATIONAL GOALS

⚽ Bobby Charlton is England's top scorer with 49 goals. Gary Lineker scored 48.

⚽ Denis Law's 30-goal tally for Scotland is a record shared with Kenny Dalglish.

⚽ Frank Stapleton is the Republic of Ireland's top scorer, with 20 goals.

⚽ When Wales beat Ireland 11–0 in 1888, Newton Heath's Doughty brothers got 6 goals. Jack scored 4 goals, while his brother Roger got 2.

⚽ Roger Byrne never scored during his thirty-three consecutive appearances for England, but might easily have done so. In 1956 he missed penalties against both Brazil and Yugoslavia.

⚽ Bryan Robson's goal for England after 27 seconds against France in the 1982 World Cup is widely reported to be the quickest goal ever scored in the finals. In fact it is only the second-fastest, as Vaclav Magek scored for Czechoslovakia after only 15 seconds against Mexico in the 1962 World Cup finals. Robson's goal also makes him England's second-quickest post-war scorer, after Tommy

Lawton's 17-second goal against Portugal in 1947.

⚽ Jack Rowley scored 6 goals in only six games for England.

⚽ Brian McClair scored 16 goals in his first twenty-five games for United, yet didn't find the net in any of his first twenty-five games for Scotland. His first Scotland goal came on his twenty-sixth appearance.

YOUNGEST INTERNATIONALS

⚽ Duncan Edwards was the youngest England player this century until Michael Owen made his international debut on 11 February 1998. Edwards was 18 years and 183 days old when he first played for his country in 1955, while Owen was aged just 18 years and 59 days.

⚽ Denis Law was Scotland's youngest post-war player when he played against Wales on 18 October 1958, aged 18 years and 236 days. He was still playing for Scotland in 1974, almost sixteen years after his debut.

⚽ In 1982 Norman Whiteside became Northern Ireland's youngest-ever player and the youngest man ever to appear in the World Cup finals. He was 17 years and 41 days old when he played against Yugoslavia, making him also the youngest ever to appear for a full international team from the British Isles.

⚽ On the day Norman Whiteside was born, 7 May 1965, his goalkeeper in the 1982 World Cup finals, Pat Jennings, was winning his seventh cap for Northern Ireland.

⚽ Four United players have played for Northern Ireland aged only seventeen:

Norman Whiteside	v. Yugoslavia	17 June 1982	17 y, 41 d
Jimmy Nicholson	v. Scotland	9 Nov. 1960	17 y, 256 d
George Best	v. Wales	15 Apr. 1964	17 y, 328 d
Sammy McIlroy	v. Spain	16 Feb. 1972	17 y, 356 d

◉ Ryan Giggs was the youngest ever player for Wales when he appeared as a substitute against West Germany on 16 October 1991, at the age of 17 years and 321 days. This record was taken by Ryan Green of Wolves when he played for Wales on 3 June 1998 at the age of 17 years and only 228 days.

◉ Johnny Giles became the Republic of Ireland's youngest ever player when he played against Sweden on 1 November 1959 at the age of 18 years and 360 days. This honour subsequently passed to Coventry City's Jimmy Holmes.

◉ Lee Sharpe was the youngest-ever England under-21 player when he played against Greece on 7 February 1989, aged 17 years and 252 days.

OLDEST INTERNATIONALS

◉ United's Billy Meredith was the oldest man ever to play for a British international side. He was 45 years and 229 days old when he played for Wales against England on 15 March 1920, 25 years after his debut in 1895.

◉ Meredith was selected for 71 consecutive internationals for Wales between 1895 and 1920, but his clubs would release him for only 51 of them.

LONGEST INTERNATIONAL CAREER

◉ Billy Meredith is thought to have had the longest international career in world soccer history – one day short of a quarter-century, from 16 March 1895 to 15 March 1920.

◉ Johnny Giles played for the Republic of Ireland for almost twenty years, from 1 November 1959 to 29 May 1979 – 19 years and 210 days.

COUNTRY BEFORE CLUB

⚽ Don Givens played for the Republic of Ireland against Denmark and Hungary in May 1969, three months before his debut for the United first team.

⚽ Brian Carey won two full caps with the Republic of Ireland in 1992 and 1993 while a reserve-team player at Old Trafford, but never played in the United first team.

⚽ Pat McGibbon had won three caps for Northern Ireland before his debut for United in September 1995.

⚽ Jovan Kirowski, a United junior player, won 17 full caps for the United States while at Old Trafford but never appeared in the United first team.

⚽ In February 1997 Philip Mulryne scored on his debut for Northern Ireland, eight months before he appeared in the United first team.

ABUNDANT INTERNATIONALS

⚽ Since the war and up to the summer of 1999, 110 United players had won 1,684 caps for the five British Isles countries – a total unsurpassed by any other club. This is made up as follows:

	Players	Caps
England	44	665
Republic of Ireland	20	342
Northern Ireland	20	299
Scotland	17	237
Wales	9	141

⚽ United have won more post-war caps for both England and the Republic of Ireland than any other club, and more caps for Northern Ireland than any other British club.

⚽ The Welsh team that played Scotland in Edinburgh in 1888 contained five Newton Heath players: Jack Doughty and his brother Roger, Jack Powell, Tom Burke and Joe Davies.

⚽ At home to West Ham United on 20 January 1973, Tommy Docherty fielded a team with eight past and future Scottish internationals: Alex Forsyth, Denis Law, Jim Holton, Martin Buchan, Willie Morgan, Ted MacDougall, Lou Macari and George Graham.

⚽ In February 1973 Scotland played against England with five United players – Martin Buchan, Alex Forsyth, George Graham, Willie Morgan and Lou Macari. They lost 5–0.

⚽ Northern Ireland fielded five United players in several matches in 1976 and 1977 – Jimmy Nicholl, Tommy Jackson, Sammy McIlroy, Chris McGrath and David McCreery. Against the Netherlands and Belgium in 1976, these five were joined by two former United players – George Best and Trevor Anderson.

⚽ The most United players to appear for England simultaneously is five, which occurred at the end of the Tornoi de France match against Italy on 4 June 1997. The five were Phil Neville, Gary Neville, Paul Scholes, Andy Cole and David Beckham. Between the moment Cole came on as substitute in the 76th minute and the time Teddy Sheringham was substituted three minutes later, England had seven players on the pitch with United connections. Paul Ince had left Old Trafford two years before, while Sheringham joined United four weeks later.

⚽ During 1960–61 the United number 3 shirt was worn by four players who won caps with the Republic of Ireland – Joe Carolan, Shay Brennan, Noel Cantwell and Tony Dunne.

⚽ From 1962 to 1964, United had two Northern Ireland international goalkeepers – Harry Gregg and Ronnie Briggs.

⚽ In three seasons – 1960–61, 1961–62 and 1978–79 –

United used nine Irish players, all of whom won caps for one or other of the Ireland teams.

⚽ The greatest number of international players United have fielded in any season is twenty, in 1998-99 – David Beckham, Henning Berg, Jesper Blomqvist, Wes Brown, Nicky Butt, Andy Cole, Jordi Cruyff, Ryan Giggs, Denis Irwin, Ronny Johnsen, Roy Keane, Philip Mulryne, Gary Neville, Phil Neville, Peter Schmeichel, Paul Scholes, Teddy Sheringham, Ole Gunnar Solskjaer, Jaap Stam and Dwight Yorke.

⚽ Eight United players appeared for England during the 1998–99 season – David Beckham, Wes Brown, Nicky Butt, Andy Cole, Gary Neville, Philip Neville, Paul Scholes and Teddy Sheringham.

⚽ Against Juventus in the European Cup on 11 September 1997 United fielded full internationals from nine different countries – Peter Schmeichel (Denmark); Gary Neville, Gary Pallister, Nicky Butt, David Beckham and Andy Cole (England); Denis Irwin (Republic of Ireland); Karel Poborsky (Czech Republic); Ronny Johnsen and Ole Gunnar Solskjaer (Norway); Eric Cantona (France); Jordi Cruyff (Netherlands); Ryan Giggs (Wales) and Brian McClair (Scotland). Only eight countries were represented on the field at any one time since McClair replaced Giggs at half-time.

⚽ United have fielded full internationals from sixteen different countries over the years. The nine countries above plus Northern Ireland (George Best and others), Yugoslavia (Nikola Jovanovic), Australia (Mark Bosnich), the United States (Eddie McIlvenny), Sweden (Jesper Blomqvist), Trinidad and Tobago (Dwight Yorke), and USSR/Ukraine (Andrei Kanchelskis). One could argue that the figure should be seventeen since Kanchelskis has played for both Russia and Ukraine.

⚽ The first time United fielded a team consisting entirely of internationals was at Leicester City on 13 November 1965 –

Gregg, Dunne, Cantwell, Crerand, Foulkes, Stiles, Best, Law, Charlton, Herd and Connelly. In the previous match, at home to Blackburn a week before, United ended the game with a full international team after Aston was substituted by Connelly.

⚽ At the start of the 1998–99 season United went for eleven consecutive matches without fielding a single player who wasn't a full international.

⚽ In the Charity Shield against Arsenal on 9 August 1998 United fielded sixteen full internationals – probably the only time this has ever happened in competitive English club football. The starting line-up was Peter Schmeichel, Gary Neville, Denis Irwin, Ronny Johnsen, Jaap Stam, David Beckham, Nicky Butt, Andy Cole, Ryan Giggs, Roy Keane and Paul Scholes. Then Ole Gunnar Solskjaer, Teddy Sheringham, Phil Neville, Jordi Cruyff and Henning Berg were allowed on as substitutes. United lost 3–0.

WORLD CUP FINALS

⚽ Five United players were in the 1970 England World Cup squad – Bobby Charlton, Brian Kidd, David Sadler, Alex Stepney and Nobby Stiles – but only Charlton actually played in Mexico.

⚽ Shay Brennan was in the original England squad of forty selected for the 1962 World Cup but failed to make the final group. He later played for the Republic of Ireland.

⚽ Thirty-five United players have appeared in the final stages of the World Cup since British countries first participated in 1950 – nine of them in 1998.

1950	England	John Aston Sr
1954	England	Roger Byrne, Tommy Taylor
1958	Northern Ireland	Harry Gregg

1958	Wales	Colin Webster
1962	England	Bobby Charlton
1966	England	Bobby Charlton, John Connelly, Nobby Stiles
1970	England	Bobby Charlton
1974	Scotland	Martin Buchan, Jim Holton, Willie Morgan
1978	Scotland	Martin Buchan, Joe Jordan, Lou Macari
1982	England	Steve Coppell, Bryan Robson, Ray Wilkins
	Northern Ireland	Norman Whiteside
	Scotland	Joe Jordan
	Yugoslavia	Nikola Jovanovic
1986	England	Bryan Robson
	Scotland	Arthur Albiston, Gordon Strachan
	Northern Ireland	Norman Whiteside
	Denmark	Jesper Olsen, Johnny Sivebaek
1990	England	Bryan Robson, Neil Webb
	Scotland	Jim Leighton
1994	Republic of Ireland	Denis Irwin, Roy Keane
1998	England	David Beckham, Gary Neville, Paul Scholes, Teddy Sheringham
	Denmark	Peter Schmeichel
	Netherlands	Jaap Stam
	Norway	Henning Berg, Ronny Johnsen, Ole Gunnar Solskjaer

⚽ Both Bobby Charlton and Bryan Robson played for England in three World Cup finals. Joe Jordan represented Scotland in three finals, the first in 1974 while he was with Leeds United.

⚽ Bobby Charlton shares with Bobby Moore the record of fourteen appearances for England in World Cup finals games.

⚽ Viv Anderson had the misfortune to travel to the 1982 and 1986 World Cup tournaments with England without getting a single game.

EUROPEAN CHAMPIONSHIP

⚽ United players appeared for four of the eight teams in the final stages of the 1992 European Championship – Neil Webb (England), Brian McClair (Scotland), Peter Schmeichel (Denmark) and Andrei Kanchelskis (CIS).

⚽ Peter Schmeichel became the first United player to win a European Championship medal when Denmark won the title in June 1992. The former United full-back Johnny Sivebaek was also in the Danish side.

⚽ The former United player Arnold Muhren won a European Championship medal with the Netherlands in June 1988, and became the oldest player ever to do so, at the age of 37 years and 23 days.

⚽ Arnold Muhren was chosen for the Dutch team both before and after his time at United, but strangely he never played for his country during his three years at Old Trafford, from 1982 to 1985.

INTERNATIONAL MANAGERS

⚽ Matt Busby was part-time manager of Scotland for several games in 1958, while his assistant at United, Jimmy Murphy, managed Wales from 1956 to 1964. Under their command both teams qualified for the 1958 World Cup finals.

⚽ Matt Busby also managed the 1948 British Olympic soccer team.

⚽ The England manager from 1946 to 1962, Walter Winterbottom, played twenty-seven games at centre-half for United before the war.

(◉) Two United managers – Tommy Docherty and Alex Ferguson – had both previously managed Scotland.

(◉) Two members of United's 1963 FA Cup-winning side – Noel Cantwell and Johnny Giles – went on to manage the Republic of Ireland.

INTERNATIONAL CAPTAINS

(◉) In 1983 United's Bryan Robson succeeded his United team-mate Ray Wilkins as England captain.

(◉) United have boasted four England captains since the war: Bobby Charlton, Ray Wilkins, Bryan Robson and Paul Ince. Peter Beardsley and David Platt captained England having previously played for United. Wilkins, Robson, Beardsley and Platt were all on United's books simultaneously during the 1982–83 season.

(◉) Paul Ince was the first black captain of England.

ODD INTERNATIONALS

(◉) Newton Heath's Joe Davies was one of four brothers who played for Wales.

(◉) United's Harold Halse played only once for England – against Austria in 1909 – but scored twice.

(◉) United's Johnny Carey played for both Northern Ireland and the Republic of Ireland. In September 1946 he played for Northern Ireland against England in Belfast, and two days later for the Republic against England in Dublin.

(◉) United's pre-war Irish goalkeeper Tommy Breen also played for both the Republic and Northern Ireland.

(◉) Charlie Mitten was chosen as 12th man for Scotland in a charity international in 1946, and the same year he played for England in a match for the Bolton Disaster Fund. But neither match was considered an official international, and he never won a full cap for either country.

⚽ Although Noel Cantwell was mainly a full-back with United, he often played at centre-forward for the Republic of Ireland. He scored 14 goals for his country, and for many years he was Ireland's leading goalscorer. This record was eventually broken by two former United players, Don Givens and then Frank Stapleton, though Cantwell still stands sixth in the Irish international goalscoring charts.

⚽ Noel Cantwell represented Ireland at both soccer and cricket.

⚽ In 1965 Shay Brennan became the first man to play for the Republic of Ireland who wasn't born in Ireland – he was a native of Manchester. Nowadays, of course, being born in Ireland hardly matters at all!

⚽ In January 1970 the future United winger Ian Storey-Moore played for England against the Netherlands, and became the only post-war England cap with a double-barrelled name.

⚽ Eddie McIlvenny, captain of the United States when they famously beat England 1–0 in the 1950 World Cup finals, played in United's first two games the following season. McIlvenny had been born in Scotland, was never a US citizen and only played briefly in the USA.

⚽ All Roger Byrne's 33 games for England between 1954 and 1957 were consecutive matches – the highest number of games by any player who only appeared in successive games.

⚽ In 1978 the future United full-back Viv Anderson became the first black player to represent England. The second was another future United player, Laurie Cunningham.

⚽ Ryan Giggs is a full international with Wales despite having played for the England schoolboy team (under the name Ryan Wilson).

⚽ When Mal Donaghy moved from United in August 1992,

it left the club with no Northern Ireland international on the books for the first time since the war. The continuity had been provided by Johnny Carey, Jackie Blanchflower, Harry Gregg, George Best, Sammy McIlroy, Jimmy Nicholl, Norman Whiteside and Donaghy, among others.

⊛ Andrei Kanchelskis was the first United player to make his home debut in an international. He played for the USSR against Argentina at Old Trafford in May 1991 before he had played there for United.

⊛ Kanchelskis won caps with three different international teams while with United – Russia, Ukraine and the USSR/CIS.

⊛ In the autumn of 1993 the Irish manager, Jack Charlton, considered selecting Steve Bruce on the basis of his Irish ancestry, but dropped the idea when he was told that the United player had won England youth caps.

⊛ Players who have won their first international caps after leaving United include Harry Baird (Northern Ireland), Stanley Ackerley (Australia), John Scott (Northern Ireland), Eamon Dimphy (Republic of Ireland), Ray Baartz (Australia), Ted MacDougall (Scotland), Ray O'Brien (Republic of Ireland), Jimmy Rimmer (England), Peter Beardsley (England), Phil Hughes (Northern Ireland), David Platt (England), Alan McLoughlin (Republic of Ireland) and Rob Savage (Wales).

⊛ The Southampton team which visited Old Trafford on 7 March 1981 contained four men who had been captain of England – Mick Channon, Dave Watson, Alan Ball and Kevin Keegan.

⊛ Andy Cole played his first four games for England under four different managers – Terry Venables, Glenn Hoddle, Howard Wilkinson and Kevin Keegan.

INEXPERIENCED INTERNATIONALS

⚽ When Henry Cockburn made his England debut against Northern Ireland in September 1946, he had only played seven League games, but this is an exceptional case – League soccer had only just resumed after the war.

⚽ Wes Brown made his debut for England against Hungary on 28 April 1999 after just fifteen League games for United (three of them as substitute) and a further seven cup matches. This was not as impressive as Arthur Milton of Arsenal, however, who made his debut for England in November 1951 after a mere twelve league matches for Arsenal in nine months.

⚽ Warren Bradley made his England debut in May 1959 after an even shorter period of *time* in the United first team – less than six months, and twenty-five appearances.

BRIEF INTERNATIONALS

⚽ Before joining United, Peter Davenport played just 17 minutes for England, as a substitute in 1985, the fourth shortest England career on record. The former United goalkeeper Jimmy Rimmer played only 45 minutes in 1976 – the seventh-briefest England career.

⚽ Ian Storey-Moore, Garry Birtles and Peter Davenport all won England caps while at Nottingham Forest, but after moving to United they never played for their country again.

⚽ The future United player Danny Wallace scored on his debut for England against Egypt in January 1986, but never won a second cap.

BROTHERS

⚽ When Gary and Philip Neville both played for England against China on 23 May 1996 they became only the ninth pair of brothers ever to appear in the same England side, and only the second set in the twentieth century after Bobby and Jackie Charlton. The Nevilles were also the youngest brothers ever to win England caps together, and the first pair from the same club since Frank and Fred Forman of Nottingham Forest in 1899.

⚽ The only other brothers from United to win international caps together were Jack and Roger Doughty, in two matches for Wales in 1888.

AMATEUR INTERNATIONALS

⚽ At one stage the United goalkeeper Mike Pinner was the most capped post-war England amateur international, with more than fifty appearances.

⚽ David Sadler played for the England amateur team at the age of sixteen, the youngest-ever England amateur cap.

⚽ Len Bradbury, Warren Bradley, Harold Hardman, Mike Pinner and John Walton all won England amateur caps while with United.

⚽ Alan Gowling played in the 1968 British Olympic soccer team.

12   FIXTURES AND FITTINGS

LEAGUE MATCHES

⚽ United had played 3,838 League games by the end of the 1998–99 season, including four test matches (the nineteenth-century equivalent of play-offs).

⚽ United's most frequent League opponents have been Arsenal, whom the Reds have met on 160 occasions. The next most common opposition have been Everton with 140 League meetings.

⚽ By the end of the 1999–2000 season United will be the only current League side whom Carlisle United have never played in the League. Carlisle's only season in the top division, 1974–75, coincided with United's one post-war season in division two. The teams have met in the FA Cup, however.

⚽ United took part in the first-ever League game staged on a Saturday night, in October 1958 against Wolverhampton Wanderers at Molineux.

HOLIDAY MATCHES

⚽ In 1958 United played League games at Old Trafford on two consecutive days, 4 and 5 April, against Sunderland and Preston North End.

⚽ In 1988 United played at Old Trafford on three consecutive days, 7, 8 and 9 May. A testimonial game against Manchester City for Arthur Albiston took place between League games against Wimbledon and Portsmouth.

⚽ On four occasions United played on three consecutive

days over the Christmas period: on 25, 26 and 27 December in 1902, 1913, 1924 and 1930.

⚽ In two years United played four League games in five days over Easter: on 9, 10, 12, 13 April 1909, and on 2, 3, 5 and 6 April 1915.

⚽ United's last Christmas Day fixture was in 1957 at home to Luton Town.

CUP DRAWS

⚽ On 7 December 1991 the League Cup and FA Cup draws were made for the first time on the same day. In the League Cup draw at lunchtime United got the worst possible tie in the fifth round – away to Leeds United, who were top of the League at the time. That evening, United were again drawn away to Leeds in the FA Cup third round. The chances of that happening were 1,763 to one.

⚽ As a result of these pairings, United were scheduled to play at Leeds United three times in eleven days in three separate competitions: on 29 December 1991 (League), 5 January 1992 (FA Cup) and 8 January (League Cup). In fact, the FA Cup game was postponed to 15 January because of bad weather, but there were still three successive away matches at Leeds over eighteen days.

⚽ During the 1991 calendar year United were paired against Leeds United three times in cup draws: the two above, and the draw in January 1991 for the 1990–91 League Cup semi-final over two legs. They won all four cup games, and thus the three ties.

⚽ In nine cases United have drawn the same opponents in both domestic cups in the same season, as follows:

1969–70 Middlesbrough	LC2	1 -0 (h)	
	FAC6	1–1 (a)	2–1 (h)
Man. City	LCSF	1–2 (a)	2–2 (h)
	FAC4	3–0 (h)	
1971–72 Stoke	LC4	1–1 (h)	0–0 (a) 1–2 (a)
	FAC6	1–1 (h)	1–2 (a)
1979–80 Spurs	LC2	1–2 (a)	3–1 (h)
	FAC3	1–1 (a)	1–2 (h)
1982–83 Arsenal	LCSF	4–2 (a)	2–1 (h)
	FACSF	2–1 (n)	
1984–85 Everton	LC3	1–2 (h)	
	FACF	1–0 (W)	
1985–86 West Ham	LC3	1–0 (h)	
	FAC5	1–1 (a)	0–2 (h)
1991–92 Leeds	LC5	3–1 (a)	
	FAC3	1–0 (a)	
1992–93 Brighton	LC2	1–1 (a)	1–0 (h)
	FAC4	1–0 (h)	

⚽ Only once have United drawn the same club twice at home in the same season – Stoke City, in 1971–72. They lost both ties in replays at Stoke.

⚽ United met Tottenham Hotspur three times in eight days between 27 January and 3 February 1968 – twice in the FA Cup and once in the League. Spoils were shared fairly evenly as the results went: FAC (h) 2–2, FAC replay (a) 0–1 and League (a) 2–1.

⚽ United met Stoke City seven times during 1971–72 – twice in the League, three times in the League Cup and twice in the FA Cup.

⚽ United also played five games at Stoke's Victoria Ground during 1971–72 – a League match against Stoke, a re-arranged home League game against West Bromwich Albion while Old Trafford was closed, and two League Cup replays and an FA Cup replay against Stoke.

⚽ Over eleven months, from 30 October 1984 to 18 September 1985, United played Everton in five competitions – the League Cup, the League, the FA Cup, the Charity Shield and the Screen Sport Super Cup.

⚽ Historically, United have met Everton in seven competitions: the above five plus the Inter Cities Fairs Cup in 1965, and the 1988 Football League Centenary Trophy.

⚽ In the autumn of 1990 United beat in cup ties the teams lying first (Liverpool), second (Arsenal), ninety-first (Wrexham) and ninety-second (Halifax Town) in the Football League. They met Wrexham in the European Cup-Winners' Cup and the other three in the League Cup.

WEMBLEY MATCHES

⚽ United visited Wembley four times during the 1993–94 season – once for the Charity Shield, once for the League Cup final, and once each for the FA Cup semi-final and final.

⚽ United also played at Wembley four times during the course of the 1983 calendar year – in the League Cup final, the FA Cup final and its replay, and the Charity Shield.

FIXTURE CONGESTION

⚽ The most matches United have played in one season is 63, on two occasions, the highly successful 1993–94 and 1998–99 campaigns. The breakdown is:

	1993–94	1998–99
League	42 games	38 games
League Cup	9 games	3 games
FA Cup	7 games	8 games
European Cup	4 games	13 games
Charity Shield	1 game	1 game

UNFAMILIAR OPPOSITION

⚽ There are twelve League clubs United have never met in competition: Barnet, Cheltenham Town, Darlington, Gillingham, Macclesfield Town, Mansfield Town, Scunthorpe United, Shrewsbury Town, Southend United, Torquay United, Wigan Athletic and Wycombe Wanderers.

⚽ Of these twelve there are eight League sides United have never met in any first-team game including friendlies: Cheltenham Town, Darlington, Gillingham, Macclesfield Town, Mansfield Town, Shrewsbury Town, Wigan Athletic and Wycombe Wanderers.

⚽ There are eight League clubs United have never visited for a first-team fixture: Cheltenham Town, Darlington, Gillingham, Macclesfield Town, Mansfield Town, Peterborough United, Wigan Athletic and Wycombe Wanderers.

⚽ There are thirteen League clubs United have never played at home: Barnet, Cheltenham Town, Darlington, Gillingham, Hartlepool United, Macclesfield Town, Mansfield Town, Scunthorpe United, Shrewsbury Town, Southend United, Torquay United, Wigan Athletic and Wycombe Wanderers. In addition, United have met Crewe Alexandra at home, but not at Old Trafford. Wigan and Hartlepool have played FA Cup replays against other clubs at Old Trafford, so there are twelve League clubs who have never visited Old

Trafford.

⚽ United have not met Crewe Alexandra in any competition since a League fixture in September 1895. This is the longest gap since any two current League clubs last played each other.

UNITED STRIPS

⚽ For their first two seasons in the Football League, Newton Heath played in red-and-white quartered jerseys and blue shorts.

⚽ From 1894 to 1896, the team wore shirts of green and gold halves.

⚽ From 1896 to 1902, Newton Heath played in white shirts and blue shorts.

⚽ Coinciding with the change of name to Manchester United in 1902, the club adopted its famous red shirts, though they have not always been maintained since.

⚽ For five seasons from 1922 to 1927 United wore white shirts with a red 'V' on both back and front, before reverting to the traditional red shirts in 1927.

⚽ During 1934, as they fought to avoid relegation to the third division, United players wore maroon-and-white hooped shirts.

⚽ Since the war United have achieved several of their most famous cup final victories playing in blue – the 1948 FA Cup, the 1968 European Cup and the 1992 League Cup.

⚽ At Southampton on 13 April 1996, United began the match playing in their alternative grey strip. At half-time, with United losing 3–0, the referee allowed the team to change into their blue-and-white reserve colours after United argued that the grey shirts made it difficult for players to spot each other. Southampton won the game 3–1.

⚽ United did not win a single competitive match playing in the alternative grey kit, which had been introduced during

the summer of 1995. Four of United's six League defeats
that season occurred in grey – at Aston Villa, Arsenal, Liverpool and Southampton, and the only point the colours
yielded came from a 1–1 draw at Nottingham Forest. The
team did win a friendly in Malaysia playing in grey, but lost
another at Celtic.

13 RED DEVILS

SENDINGS-OFF

:soccer: The only men ever sent off in FA or League Cup finals have been United players – Kevin Moran in the 1985 FA Cup final, and Andrei Kanchelskis in the 1994 League Cup final.

:soccer: On 20 September 1995 Pat McGibbon was sent off after 51 minutes of his United debut, in a League Cup match against York City. He left United in July 1997 having never played for the first team again.

:soccer: United's Liam O'Brien was sent off after only 85 seconds at Southampton in January 1987. This remains the quickest-ever dismissal in the top division.

:soccer: Jim Holton was sent off twice in his first nine games for United.

:soccer: In September 1998 Nicky Butt became the third United player to be dismissed in two successive matches. The details are:

Jimmy Turnbull	Aston Villa (h)	16 Oct. 1909
	Sheffield United (a)	23 Oct. 1909
Eric Cantona	Swindon Town (a)	19 Mar. 1994
	Arsenal (a)	22 Mar. 1994
Nicky Butt	Barcelona (ECC)(h)	16 Sept. 1998
	Arsenal (a)	20 Sept. 1998

:soccer: In May 1908 three United players, including Dick Duckworth and Ernie Thomson, were sent off during a friendly against Ferencváros in Budapest, but the referee later changed his mind and allowed them to continue playing.

⚽ The former United captain Frank Barson was reputedly sent off twelve times during his career.

⚽ In August 1959, eighteen months after the Munich disaster, United returned to Germany to play a friendly against Bayern Munich, only to have two players sent off – Joe Carolan and Albert Quixall. United still won 2–1.

⚽ Noel Cantwell and Harry Gregg were both sent off in a reserve match at Burnley on 13 February 1965.

⚽ When Pat Crerand was sent off at Ferencvaros in June 1965 it was said to be United's tenth sending-off in twenty months, though this was counting reserve games.

⚽ At Maine Road on 13 March 1974, United's Lou Macari and Manchester City's Mike Doyle were dismissed together. Both players refused to leave the pitch, and to resolve matters the referee Clive Thomas had to take both teams off for five minutes. The game eventually resumed without either player.

⚽ The 1986–87 season saw three opposing players sent off at Old Trafford in the space of nine games – Paul Rocastle (Arsenal), Chris Fairclough (Nottingham Forest) and Brian Gayle (Wimbledon).

⚽ Harry Gregg and Peter Schmeichel are the only United goalkeepers thought to have been sent off in first-team fixtures since the war – Gregg at home to Blackburn Rovers in November 1965, and Schmeichel at home to Charlton Athletic in the FA Cup in March 1994.

⚽ United suffered four sendings-off during the course of five matches in March 1994.

⚽ Eric Cantona was sent off five times in fifteen months between November 1993 and January 1995.

⚽ United's most sendings-off in one season was seven in 1993–94 – as many as had been dismissed over the previous seven-and-a-half years. A further six players were dismissed the following season.

⚽ Over the course of just fourteen matches during 1995, Roy Keane was sent off three times.

⚽ On 5 June 1999, in a European Championship match against Sweden, Paul Scholes became the first England player to be sent off at Wembley.

CAUTIONS

⚽ When Notts County visited Old Trafford on Boxing Day 1984, nine of the visiting team were booked – seven of them in one go for refusing to move back ten yards at a free kick. In a previous Boxing Day game, in 1971, five Coventry City players were booked for the same offence.

⚽ The only 'booking' of Bobby Charlton's club career was for wasting time during the 1967 Charity Shield game against Tottenham Hotspur. Later the referee decided not to report the caution when he realized United had been losing 3–2 at the time.

SUSPENSIONS

⚽ In 1915 an FA commission decided that United's 2–0 victory over Liverpool in April that year had been fixed, but the result was allowed to stand. Three United players, including Sandy Turnbull and Enoch West, were suspended for life, along with four Liverpool men, but after the war the suspensions were quashed. As a result of this fixed match United finished the season one point ahead of relegated Chelsea, but many argued that United should have gone down instead. When football resumed after the First World War, the Football League resolved the issue by extending the top division by two clubs.

⚽ In 1928 United's former captain Frank Barson was suspended for the rest of the season after being sent off playing for Watford against Fulham. This was the longest-ever suspension in League history up to that point.

◉ In 1969, the FA found United guilty of making irregular payments, and banned them from playing friendlies against European teams.

◉ In 1971 George Best escaped suspension when United used TV film as evidence at an FA hearing – the first time a player was acquitted in this way.

◉ In 1971 the FA closed Old Trafford for the first two matches of the 1971–72 season because a knife had been thrown on to the pitch during a game. United played the two fixtures at Liverpool and Stoke City instead, and beat Arsenal and West Bromwich Albion by 3–1 in each case.

◉ In December 1971 the United reserve player Kevin Lewis received what was then a post-war record suspension of five months for attacking a referee. Lewis never appeared in the United first team, but later played for Stoke City.

◉ In 1977 United were forced to play a European Cup Winners' Cup home leg against St Etienne at Plymouth Argyle's ground, Home Park, as a punishment for bad behaviour by United fans during the first leg. This was a reprieve, as UEFA had initially expelled United from the competition. United won the match 2–0.

◉ In 1990 United had one League point deducted after a brawl erupted during the home defeat by Arsenal that October. Arsenal had two points deducted. This was the first time League sides had been disciplined in this way. Arsenal still went on to win the League.

◉ In February 1995 Eric Cantona was suspended by the FA for eight months for attacking a spectator after being sent off at Crystal Palace in January.

◉ The Frenchman's suspension was widely blamed for

United's failure to retain the Double in 1995. The following season, however, a reformed Eric Cantona was captain when United won both the League title and the FA Cup for a second time, and it was generally acknowledged that his return and vital winning goals had made all the difference. Yet strangely enough, over the two seasons United had actually picked up more points per game when Cantona wasn't playing than when he was.

14 RED HEADS

⚽ In terms of honours, Sir Alex Ferguson is now indisputably the most successful manager in United history, having won twelve major trophies in thirteen years, compared with the eight won by Sir Matt Busby in his twenty-five years.

⚽ The comparative table is:

	Sir Matt Busby	Sir Alex Ferguson
League titles	1952, 1956, 1957, 1965, 1967	1993, 1994, 1996, 1997, 1999
European Cup	1968	1999
European Cup-Winners' Cup		1991
FA Cup	1948, 1963	1990, 1994, 1996, 1999
League Cup		1992

⚽ The next most successful United manager was Ernest Mangnall who won two League titles (1908 and 1911) and the FA Cup (1909) during his nine years with the club.

⚽ Ferguson's twelve trophies at Old Trafford compare with the thirteen pieces of silverware won by Bob Paisley at Liverpool.

⚽ Adding Ferguson's record with Aberdeen, the United manager has now won twenty-one major trophies in England and Scotland, still well short of the twenty-six trophies

Jock Stein won with Dunfermline and Celtic.

⊙ The Manager of the Year award has gone to Old Trafford six times – to Matt Busby in 1968, and to Alex Ferguson in 1993, 1994, 1996, 1997 and 1999. Ferguson is now one behind the former Liverpool manager, Bob Paisley, who won the award six times.

⊙ When Preston North End visited Old Trafford in April 1958 their two wing-halves were the future United managers Frank O'Farrell and Tommy Docherty.

⊙ Although they are very different characters, and one replaced the other as United manager in December 1972, Frank O'Farrell is godfather to one of Tommy Docherty's sons.

⊙ Tommy Docherty had previously appointed his successor at United, Dave Sexton, as assistant coach at Chelsea when Docherty was manager at Stamford Bridge in the mid-1960s.

⊙ Dave Sexton followed Tommy Docherty as manager at three different clubs – Chelsea, Queen's Park Rangers and United.

⊙ In the early 1990s Dave Sexton served as coach at Aston Villa under the man who succeeded him at Old Trafford, Ron Atkinson. So at different points in his career Sexton has worked for the men who both preceded and succeeded him as United manager.

⊙ Alex Ferguson and Wilf McGuinness both had sons who played for United. Darren Ferguson made his first-team debut in 1991, but Paul McGuinness, in the mid-1980s, only reached the reserves. Sir Matt Busby's son, Sandy, played for Blackburn Rovers reserves at Old Trafford in the late fifties, while Busby's son-in-law, Don Gibson, played for United. Tommy Docherty's son, Peter, played for United in the 1982 FA Youth Cup final.

⊙ Jimmy Murphy's son Nick never quite made the United first team. He came very close when he was twice named as substitute but not used – at Liverpool on 12 October 1968, and at home to Sunderland on 18 January 1969.

⚽ Both Tommy Docherty's assistant managers had sons who played for the United junior sides in the mid-1980s – Danny Crerand, the son of Pat, and Tommy Cavanagh junior.

⚽ Matt Busby selected Tommy Docherty for the Scotland team in 1958, and then proposed him as United manager in 1972.

⚽ Ernest Mangnall managed United from 1903 to 1912 – one of the most successful periods in the club's history – and then switched to Manchester City for the next twelve years.

⚽ Bobby Charlton became manager of Preston North End in May 1973, three days before his brother Jackie became manager of Middlesbrough.

⚽ As a player with Luton Town, West Ham United, Leyton Orient, Brighton & Hove Albion and Crystal Palace, Dave Sexton never played against United.

⚽ In more than five years at Old Trafford, Ron Atkinson managed United in eight Manchester derbies but was never on the losing side.

⚽ Alex Ferguson is the only manager to have won the three main Scottish trophies – with Aberdeen – and each of their English equivalents – with United. Indeed, he is also the only manager to win both the English and Scottish League titles.

⚽ In 1995 Alex Ferguson overtook Ernest Mangnall to become the second-longest serving manager in United history, after Sir Matt Busby. In November 1998 Ferguson completed twelve years in charge at Old Trafford. Busby served for almost twenty-five years.

⚽ By the summer of 1999 there was only one currently-serving League manger who had lasted longer than Sir Alex Ferguson. Dario Gradi was appointed manager of Crewe Alexandra in June 1983.

☉ Clarence Hilditch was United's only-ever player-manager, from October 1926 to April 1927. After his resignation he continued playing for United for another five years.

☉ The United manager from 1927 to 1931, Herbert Bamlett, had previously been a referee, and in 1914, at the age of thirty-two, he became the youngest-ever FA Cup final referee.

☉ The United chairman from 1951 to 1965, Harold Hardman, had a remarkable career. An amateur player who won an Olympic gold medal for soccer in 1908, he also gained four full England caps. He helped Everton win the FA Cup in 1906 and made four appearances for United in 1908. Appointed a United director in 1912, Hardman served almost continuously on the Old Trafford board for fifty-three years.

☉ Tommy Docherty's assistant at United, Tommy Cavanagh Senior, had an unfortunate soccer history. He suffered relegation with four different clubs he played for – Preston North End, Huddersfield Town, Doncaster Rovers and Bristol City. Cavanagh was then coach with Nottingham Forest when they were relegated in 1972. He arrived at Old Trafford in 1973, and a year later United went down to division two.

☉ The former Conservative Prime Minister Arthur Balfour was a vice-president of United during the early years of the twentieth century.

15 UNITED TRANSFERS

MOST EXPENSIVE

⚽ Since the war, United's most expensive transfer purchases have progressively been:

John Downie	£20,000	Bradford P.A.	Mar. 1949
Johnny Berry	£25,000	Birmingham	Aug. 1951
Tommy Taylor	£29,999	Barnsley	Mar. 1953
*Albert Quixall	£45,000	Sheffield Wed.	Sept. 1958
*Denis Law	£115,000	Torino	Aug. 1962
Martin Buchan	£125,000	Aberdeen	Mar. 1972
Ian Storey-Moore	£180,000	Nottm. Forest	Mar. 1972
Ted MacDougall	£200,000	Bournemouth	Sept. 1972
Joe Jordan	£350,000	Leeds	Jan. 1978
*Gordon McQueen	£450,000	Leeds	Feb. 1978
Ray Wilkins	£700,000	Chelsea	Aug. 1979
Garry Birtles	£1,250,000	Nottm. Forest	Oct. 1980
*Bryan Robson	£1,500,000	WBA	Oct. 1981
Mark Hughes	£1,600,000	Barcelona	July 1988
*Gary Pallister	£2,300,000	Middlesbrough	Aug. 1989
*Roy Keane	£3,750,000	Nottm. Forest	July 1993
*Andy Cole	£7,000,000	Newcastle	Jan. 1995
Jaap Stam	£10,600,000	PSV Eindhoven	June 1998
Dwight Yorke	£12,600,000	Aston Villa	Aug. 1998

* The most expensive purchase then made by an English club.

⚽ When United paid Queen's Park Rangers £11,000 for Reg

Allen in 1950, it was a British record for a goalkeeper.

⚽ In March 1953 Matt Busby signed Tommy Taylor from Barnsley for £29,999. He had asked Barnsley to knock a pound off the price as he feared the high figure might go to Taylor's head.

⚽ Denis Law's move to United from Torino in August 1962 for £115,000 was the first British transfer above £100,000.

⚽ United's substitutes' bench for the 1999 FA Cup final cost the club £31.1m, almost twice as much as the team that started the match: Jaap Stam, £10.6m, Jesper Blomqvist, £4.4m, Teddy Sheringham, £3.5m and Dwight Yorke £12.6m. But the substitute goalkeeper Raimond van der Gouw cost nothing.

TRANSFER SALES

⚽ United's biggest transfer sales since the war have progressively been:

Joe Walton	£12,000	Preston	Mar. 1948
Johnny Morris	£25,000	Derby	Mar. 1949
Johnny Giles	£34,000	Leeds	Aug. 1963
John Connelly	£40,000	Blackburn	Sept. 1966
Alan Gowling	£60,000	Huddersfield	June 1972
Ted MacDougall	£170,000	West Ham	Mar. 1973
Gordon Hill	£275,000	Derby	Apr. 1978
Brian Greenhoff	£350,000	Leeds	Aug. 1979
Andy Ritchie	£500,000	Brighton	Oct. 1980
Ray Wilkins	£1,400,000	AC Milan	June 1984
Mark Hughes	£1,800,000	Barcelona	Aug. 1986
Dion Dublin	£1,950,000	Coventry	Sept. 1994
Paul Ince	£6,000,000	Inter Milan	June 1995

MANCHESTER MOVES

⚽ At least thirty-four players have appeared for the first teams of both Manchester United and Manchester City. Three of the most famous played for Manchester City first, then moved to United and finally returned to City: Billy Meredith, Denis Law and Peter Barnes. Harry Rowley did the reverse, first playing for United, then City, and later United again.

⚽ Apart from the above, the following also played for City and later for United: William Douglas, Daniel Hurst, Fred Williams, Bert Read, Sandy Turnbull, Jimmy Bannister, Herbert Burgess, George Livingstone, Bill Ridding, Len Langford and Wyn Davies.

⚽ As well as Meredith, Law, Barnes and Rowley, the following also played for United and later for City: Bob Milarvie, Adam Carson, Joe Cassidy, Frank Barrett, Hugh Morgan, John Christie, Frank Buckley, Herbert Broomfield, Mick Hamill, Frank Knowles, Wilf Woodcock, George Albinson, Billy Dale, Brian Kidd, Peter Bodak, John Gidman, Sammy McIlroy, Peter Beardsley and Terry Cooke.

⚽ The most expensive transfer between the two clubs was when United sold Terry Cooke to City for £600,000 in April 1999. The most expensive transfer from City to United was Tony Coton who cost £500,000 in January 1996, though he never played for the United first team and moved to Sunderland six months later. Coton and Wyn Davies are the only players to move directly from City to United since 1934.

⚽ Peter Beardsley is the only player to have played for both Manchester United and City – albeit briefly in both cases – and for Liverpool and Everton. John Gidman was on the books of all four clubs but never played in the Liverpool first team.

BAD DEALS

⚽ Forward Terry Gibson cost £630,000 from Coventry in 1986 and was sold for £200,000 to Wimbledon eighteen months later, a total outlay of £430,000 for just 1 goal in twenty-three games.

⚽ Garry Birtles cost £1.25 million from Nottingham Forest in 1980, and was sold back to Forest less than two years later for £275,000 – nearly a million pounds for 12 goals in sixty-four appearances.

⚽ United sold Peter Beardsley to Vancouver Whitecaps for £250,000 in 1982. Four years later Liverpool bought him from Newcastle United for £1,900,000 – then a record British transfer fee.

ODD TRANSFERS

⚽ It is said that Hugh McLenahan's transfer from Stockport County to United in 1927 was secured by the donation of three freezers of ice-cream to the County bazaar.

⚽ Matt Busby didn't buy anyone between 1953 and 1957. In Busby's first thirteen years before Munich he bought only sixteen players, four of whom were goalkeepers.

⚽ From 1964 to 1972, United bought only three players in eight years – Alex Stepney, Willie Morgan and Ian Ure.

⚽ Alex Stepney joined United from Chelsea in 1966, having played just one game for Chelsea since his transfer from Millwall 112 days before.

⚽ In September 1966 Tommy Docherty sold George Graham from Chelsea to Arsenal in a deal that also involved Tommy Baldwin moving from Highbury to Stamford Bridge. Later, in the 1970s, both players served under Docherty at United.

⚽ Between December 1972 and April 1973, Tommy Docherty bought seven players in four months.

⚽ The £1.5 million United had to pay Nottingham Forest for

Neil Webb in July 1989 was the first time a tribunal had decided on a fee of more than £1 million.

⚽ Only three post-war players have had two spells with United:

Mark Hughes	1983–86 and 1988–95
Les Sealey	1990–91 and 1993–94
Mark Bosnich	1990–91 and 1999–

⚽ In 1995 and 1996 three successive United transfer acquisitions were goalkeepers – Nick Culkin, Tony Coton and Raimond van der Gouw.

16 RED ARMY

AVERAGE CROWDS

⚽ United's average home League gate of 57,759 in 1967–68 remains an all-time English record, though this is likely to be broken when the capacity of Old Trafford is extended to 67,400 over the next two to three years. Nine League games at Old Trafford in 1967–68 saw crowds of more than 60,000 and only one fixture – against Southampton – attracted a crowd of less than 50,000.

⚽ In both 1997–98 and 1998–99 United attracted more than 55,000 for every home League game. No other club in English history has ever managed to attract more than 50,000 for every home League match in a season.

⚽ A total of 3,018,154 watched United during 1967–68, which was said to be a world record for one season at the time.

⚽ In the second division in 1974–75 United attracted an average home crowd of 48,389 – over 2,000 more than the best-supported first-division side that season, Liverpool.

⚽ In only one season since the war, 1954–55, have Manchester City attracted more home support than United.

⚽ In twenty-nine of the last thirty-four seasons United have attracted the highest home crowds in the League. Liverpool achieved higher gates in the remaining five years: 1970–71, 1971–72, 1987–88, 1988–89, and in 1992–93 when the Old Trafford capacity was restricted by redevelopment work.

⚽ Since League football began in 1888, United have

achieved the highest average crowds in thirty-two seasons, more than for any other club. The next best are Everton, who have enjoyed the strongest home support thirteen times, and Arsenal, in twelve seasons.

⚽ Away from home, United were the most popular League visitors for ten seasons running, from 1963 to 1973.

⚽ Historically, United have been the most attractive visitors in twenty-seven seasons in all, again more than any other club. Liverpool and Arsenal have both been the most popular visitors in sixteen seasons each.

HOME ATTENDANCES

⚽ United boast the biggest ever League crowd, 81,962 for the home fixture against Arsenal on 17 January 1948, though this was played at Maine Road because of war damage to the Old Trafford ground.

⚽ United's best home attendance in all competitions was 82,771 for the fourth-round FA Cup tie at Maine Road against Bradford Park Avenue in January 1949.

⚽ The biggest crowd at Old Trafford was 76,962 for the FA Cup semi-final between Wolverhampton Wanderers and Grimsby Town in March 1939. This was also the last occasion on which Old Trafford housed more than 70,000.

⚽ United's best Old Trafford crowd was 70,504, against Aston Villa on 27 December 1920.

⚽ United's best post-war Old Trafford gate was 66,350, for an FA Cup fifth-round tie against Sheffield Wednesday in February 1960.

⚽ United's best post-war Old Trafford League crowd was 66,124, against Nottingham Forest in February 1958, the first home League game after Munich.

⚽ United's best home European crowd was 75,598, against
Borussia Dortmund at Maine Road in the European Cup in

October 1956.

⚽ United's best Old Trafford European crowd was 65,000, against Real Madrid in the European Cup semi-final in April 1957.

⚽ United's best second-division crowd – home or away – was 60,585, at home to Sunderland in November 1974.

⚽ United also boast the best League Cup gate for a match outside Wembley: 63,418 watched the 2–2 draw with Manchester City in the second leg of the semi-final at Old Trafford in December 1969.

⚽ The lowest United crowd at Old Trafford was 3,507, for the visit of Southampton in September 1931, the first home game of the season. Less than four months later, on Christmas Day 1931, United had a crowd almost ten times as large – 33,123 against Wolverhampton Wanderers – while 37,012 saw the home game against Charlton Athletic the following March.

⚽ United's worst post-war home gate was 8,456, for the League visit of Stoke City in February 1947. The match took place at Maine Road on a Wednesday afternoon.

⚽ United's lowest post-war Old Trafford crowd was 11,381, for the Charity Shield against Newcastle United in September 1952.

⚽ United's worst post-war League gate at Old Trafford was 11,968, against Fulham in April 1950.

⚽ The lowest crowd in League history is widely reputed to have been at Old Trafford in May 1921. Officially 13 people are supposed to have attended the second division match between Stockport County and Leicester City. The game had been switched from Edgeley Park to Old Trafford at short notice and played two hours after United's final home League fixture against Derby County. But the true attendance is reckoned to be well over a thousand, since many stayed on after the earlier game.

⚽ The most recent Old Trafford crowd of more than 60,000 was against Leeds United on 12 March 1977, with 60,612 present.

⚽ United's gate of 50,028 against Arsenal on 20 March 1996 was the first crowd of more than 50,000 at any English club ground since 53,000 attended the fateful FA Cup semi-final at Hillsborough in April 1989, when 96 people died.

⚽ On Saturday 7 October 1995, 21,502 people watched a reserve match against Leeds United at Old Trafford in which Eric Cantona was playing only his second game after his eight-month suspension from football. This was a bigger crowd than at any ground in the lower three divisions that day.

⚽ United's top four home League attendances during 1993–94 differed only by six – Liverpool 44,751, Everton 44,750, Wimbledon 44,748 and Chelsea 44,745.

⚽ The attendance of 81,565 at Maine Road for United's FA Cup fifth round game against Yeovil on 12 February 1949 was the highest-ever crowd to see a non-League team in the FA Cup.

AWAY ATTENDANCES

⚽ United's biggest-ever crowd was probably the 125,000 who saw the second leg of the European Cup semi-final in Real Madrid's Bernabeu stadium in May 1968.

⚽ United's best post-war away League crowd was 72,077 at Everton in September 1957. This is also thought to be a League record for a midweek match.

⚽ United's lowest gate in a competitive match since the First World War was probably 2,750 at Nelson for a second-division game in March 1924.

⚽ United's lowest post-war crowd for a competitive game was 4,670 for the League Cup second round at Bradford City in November 1960.

⚽ United's worst post-war away League crowd was 8,966 at Oxford United in May 1988.

⚽ United's worst European crowd was 6,537 at Djurgårdens in the Inter Cities Fairs Cup in September 1964.

SIGNS OF FANATICISM

⚽ United's League match at Arsenal in March 1967 was watched by 28,000 on closed-circuit TV screens at Old Trafford – the first time that pictures of a game had been relayed in this way.

⚽ United sold 74,680 programmes for the World Club Championship home game against Estudiantes in 1968, which was said to be a record for any match other than a cup final.

⚽ 260,000 programmes were sold for the 1968 European Cup final.

⚽ United's away match at Wimbledon after clinching the championship in May 1993 probably saw the greatest ever ratio of away fans to home supporters. Of the 30,115 crowd, which exceeded Wimbledon's previous home record by 11,000, around 24,000 (some say more) were estimated to have been United fans. It was more than double Wimbledon's best other gate that season, and accounted for 17 per cent of the London club's total home League attendance for 1992–93.

⚽ United are responsible for the all-time record crowds at eight League clubs: Bournemouth, Hartlepool United, Hull City, Nottingham Forest, Southampton, Watford, Wimbledon and Wrexham. Arsenal are the only other club to have attracted the record crowd at eight clubs.

17 YOUNG UNITED

⚽ United have won the Youth Cup a record eight times. The next most successful club are Arsenal, with four wins. United have appeared in a record eleven finals.

⚽ United won the first five Youth Cups from 1953 to 1957. They won three of the two-legged finals by six-goal margins, beating Wolverhampton Wanderers 9–3 in 1953, West Bromwich Albion 7–1 in 1955 and West Ham United 8–2 in 1957.

⚽ Five players won a record three FA Youth Cup medals with United: Eddie Colman and Duncan Edwards (1953, 1954 and 1955) and Bobby Charlton, Wilf McGuinness and Tony Hawksworth (1954, 1955 and 1956).

⚽ United were unbeaten in FA Youth Cup ties until 1958, when they lost in the semi-final to the eventual winners, Wolverhampton Wanderers.

⚽ United's record score in the Youth Cup is 23–0 against Nantwich Town in the second round in 1952–53. In the early years United frequently scored ten goals or more in Youth Cup games, as follows:

1952–53	23–0	v. Nantwich Town (h)
1955–56	11–1	v. Bexleyheath (h)
1959–60	14–0	v. Morecambe (h)
1961–62	10–1	v. Wigan Athletic (a, but switched to OT)
1962–63	15–0	v. Bradford City (h)
1963–64	14–1	v. Barrow (h)

United's best away score in the Youth Cup is 9–0 at Derby County in January 1984.

Between April 1954 and April 1956 United won seventeen successive Youth Cup matches.

United went 43 games unbeaten from the start of the Youth Cup in 1952 until they lost the home leg of the semi-final 3–2 to Southampton in April 1956 (but the result hardly mattered as they'd already won the away leg 5–2).

United's worst defeat in the Youth Cup was 5–0 at Everton in 1964–65, immediately after winning the trophy in 1964. United's worst home defeat in the Youth Cup was 4–1 to West Bromwich Albion in 1975–76.

LATER SUCCESS

The United team which won the Youth Cup in 1991–92 was arguably the most successful of all time. Of the fourteen players who won the two-legged final against Crystal Palace, only three never played for the United first team. Seven of the team have since become full internationals – Gary Neville, David Beckham, Nicky Butt, Simon Davies, Rob Savage, Ryan Giggs and Keith Gillespie.

Only three of the 1953–54 Youth Cup side failed to make the first team, while Duncan Edwards, Bobby Charlton, Wilf McGuinness and David Pegg all played for England.

Of the 1954–55 winning team only four never played for the first team, and Edwards, Charlton, McGuinness and Shay Brennan became internationals.

CROWDS

The 1993 FA Youth Cup final games against Leeds United drew 61,599 spectators, which is probably a record aggregate attendance for the competition. 30,562 attended the first leg at Old Trafford on 11 May 1993, and 31,037 were at the second game three days later. This is almost 15,000 more than United's previous record aggregate, for the 1954 final against Wolves.

⚽ The highest crowd for a single Youth Cup match was probably the 35,949 who saw United's home semi-final against Blackburn Rovers in April 1959.

⚽ In March 1956 a fifth round Youth Cup game against Bexleyheath attracted a crowd of 23,850. United won 11–1.

APPENDIX 1
UNITED IN THE LEAGUE, 1892–93 TO 1998–99

| | | Home | | | | | Away | | | | | | |
	P	W	D	L	F	A	W	D	L	F	A	Pts	Pos
First division													
1892–93	30	6	3	6	39	35	0	3	12	11	50	18	16th
1893–94	30	5	2	8	29	33	1	0	14	7	39	14	16th
Second division													
1894–95	30	9	6	0	52	18	6	2	7	26	26	38	3rd
1895–96	30	12	2	1	48	15	3	1	11	18	42	33	6th
1896–97	30	11	4	0	37	10	6	1	8	19	24	39	2nd
1897–98	30	11	2	2	42	10	5	4	6	22	25	38	4th
1898–99	34	12	4	1	51	14	7	1	9	16	29	43	4th
1899–1900	34	15	1	1	44	11	5	3	9	19	16	44	4th
1900–01	34	11	3	3	31	9	3	1	13	11	29	32	10th
1901–02	34	10	2	5	27	12	1	4	12	11	41	28	15th
1902–03	34	9	4	4	32	15	6	4	7	21	23	38	5th
1903–04	34	14	2	1	42	14	6	6	5	23	19	48	3rd
1904–05	34	16	0	1	60	10	8	5	4	21	20	53	3rd
1905–06	38	15	3	1	55	13	13	3	3	35	15	62	2nd
First division													
1906–07	38	10	6	3	33	15	7	2	10	20	41	42	8th
1907–08	38	15	1	3	43	19	8	5	6	38	29	52	1st

APPENDIX 1 – UNITED IN THE LEAGUE

		Home					Away						
	P	W	D	L	F	A	W	D	L	F	A	Pts	Pos
1908–09	38	10	3	6	37	33	5	4	10	21	35	37	13th
1909–10	38	14	2	3	41	20	5	5	9	28	41	45	5th
1910–11	38	14	4	1	47	18	8	4	7	25	22	52	1st
1911–12	38	9	5	5	29	19	4	6	9	16	41	37	13th
1912–13	38	13	3	3	41	14	6	5	8	28	29	46	4th
1913–14	38	8	4	7	27	23	7	2	10	25	39	36	14th
1914–15	38	8	6	5	27	19	1	6	12	19	43	30	18th
1915–19 No competition													
1919–20	42	6	8	7	20	17	7	6	8	34	33	40	12th
1920–21	42	9	4	8	34	26	6	6	9	30	42	40	13th
1921–22	42	7	7	7	25	26	1	5	15	16	47	28	22nd

Second division

	P	W	D	L	F	A	W	D	L	F	A	Pts	Pos
1922–23	42	10	6	5	25	17	7	8	6	26	19	48	4th
1923–24	42	10	7	4	37	15	3	7	11	15	29	40	14th
1924–25	42	17	3	1	40	6	6	8	7	17	17	57	2nd

First division

	P	W	D	L	F	A	W	D	L	F	A	Pts	Pos
1925–26	42	12	4	5	40	26	7	2	12	26	47	44	9th
1926–27	42	9	8	4	29	19	4	6	11	23	45	40	15th
1927–28	42	12	6	3	51	27	4	1	16	21	53	39	18th
1928–29	42	8	8	5	32	23	6	5	10	34	53	41	12th
1929–30	42	11	4	6	39	34	4	4	13	28	54	38	17th
1930–31	42	6	6	9	30	37	1	2	18	23	78	22	22nd

Second division

	P	W	D	L	F	A	W	D	L	F	A	Pts	Pos
1931–32	42	12	3	6	44	31	5	5	11	27	41	42	12th
1932–33	42	11	5	5	40	24	4	8	9	31	44	43	6th
1933–34	42	9	3	9	29	33	5	3	13	30	52	34	20th
1934–35	42	16	2	3	50	21	7	2	12	26	34	50	5th
1935–36	42	16	3	2	55	16	6	9	6	30	27	56	1st

	P	W	D	L	F	A	W	D	L	F	A	Pts	Pos
			Home					*Away*					

First division

	P	W	D	L	F	A	W	D	L	F	A	Pts	Pos
1936–37	42	8	9	4	29	26	2	3	16	26	52	32	21st

Second division

| 1937–38 | 42 | 15 | 3 | 3 | 50 | 18 | 7 | 6 | 8 | 32 | 32 | 53 | 2nd |

First division

| 1938–39 | 42 | 7 | 9 | 5 | 30 | 20 | 4 | 7 | 10 | 27 | 45 | 38 | 14th |

1939–46 No competition

	P	W	D	L	F	A	W	D	L	F	A	Pts	Pos
1946–47	42	17	3	1	61	19	5	9	7	34	35	56	2nd
1947–48	42	11	7	3	50	27	8	7	6	31	21	52	2nd
1948–49	42	11	7	3	40	20	10	4	7	37	24	53	2nd
1949–50	42	11	5	5	42	20	7	9	5	27	24	50	4th
1950–51	42	14	4	3	42	16	10	4	7	32	24	56	2nd
1951–52	42	15	3	3	55	21	8	8	5	40	31	57	1st
1952–53	42	11	5	5	35	30	7	5	9	34	42	46	8th
1953–54	42	11	6	4	41	27	7	6	8	32	31	48	4th
1954–55	42	12	4	5	44	30	8	3	10	40	44	47	5th
1955–56	42	18	3	0	51	20	7	7	7	32	31	60	1st
1956–57	42	14	4	3	55	25	14	4	3	48	29	64	1st
1957–58	42	10	4	7	45	31	6	7	8	40	44	43	9th
1958–59	42	14	4	3	58	27	10	3	8	45	39	55	2nd
1959–60	42	13	3	5	53	30	6	4	11	49	50	45	7th
1960–61	42	14	5	2	58	20	4	4	13	30	56	45	7th
1961–62	42	10	3	8	44	31	5	6	10	28	44	39	15th
1962–63	42	6	6	9	36	38	6	4	11	31	43	34	19th
1963–64	42	15	3	3	54	19	8	4	9	36	43	53	2nd
1964–65	42	16	4	1	52	13	10	5	6	37	26	61	1st
1965–66	42	12	8	1	50	20	6	7	8	34	39	51	4th
1966–67	42	17	4	0	51	13	7	8	6	33	32	60	1st
1967–68	42	15	2	4	49	21	9	6	6	40	34	56	2nd
1968–69	42	13	5	3	38	18	2	7	12	19	35	42	11th
1969–70	42	8	9	4	37	27	6	8	7	29	34	45	8th

	P	W	D	L	F	A	W	D	L	F	A	Pts	Pos
		Home					*Away*						
1970–71	42	9	6	6	29	24	7	5	9	36	42	43	8th
1971–72	42	13	2	6	39	26	6	8	7	30	35	48	8th
1972–73	42	9	7	5	24	19	3	6	12	20	41	37	18th
1973–74	42	7	7	7	23	20	3	5	13	15	28	32	21st

Second division

1974–75	42	17	3	1	45	12	9	6	6	21	18	61	1st

First division

1975–76	42	16	4	1	40	13	7	6	8	28	29	56	3rd
1976–77	42	12	6	3	41	22	6	5	10	30	40	47	6th
1977–78	42	9	6	6	32	23	7	4	10	35	40	42	10th
1978–79	42	9	7	5	29	25	6	8	7	31	38	45	9th
1979–80	42	17	3	1	43	8	7	7	7	22	27	58	2nd
1980–81	42	9	11	1	30	14	6	7	8	21	22	48	8th
1981–82	42	12	6	3	27	9	10	6	5	32	20	78	3rd
1982–83	42	14	7	0	39	10	5	6	10	17	28	70	3rd
1983–84	42	14	3	4	43	18	6	11	4	28	23	74	4th
1984–85	42	13	6	2	47	13	9	4	8	30	34	76	4th
1985–86	42	12	5	4	35	12	10	5	6	35	24	76	4th
1986–87	42	13	3	5	38	18	1	11	9	14	27	56	11th
1987–88	40	14	5	1	41	17	9	7	4	30	21	81	2nd
1988–89	38	10	5	4	27	13	3	7	9	18	22	51	11th
1989–90	38	8	6	5	26	14	5	3	11	20	33	48	13th
1990–91	38	11	4	4	34	17	5	8	6	24	28	59*	6th
1991–92	42	12	7	2	34	13	9	8	4	29	20	78	2nd
1992–93	42	14	5	2	39	14	10	7	4	28	17	84	1st
1993–94	42	14	6	1	39	13	13	5	3	41	25	92	1st
1994–95	42	16	4	1	42	4	10	6	5	35	24	88	2nd
1995–96	38	15	4	0	36	9	10	3	6	37	26	82	1st
1996–97	38	12	5	2	38	17	9	7	3	38	27	75	1st

| | P | | Home | | | | | Away | | | | | |
		W	D	L	F	A	W	D	L	F	A	Pts	Pos
1997–98	38	13	4	2	42	9	10	4	5	31	17	77	2nd
1998–99	38	14	4	1	45	18	8	9	2	35	19	79	1st

Since 1981–82, three points have been awarded for a win.

* 1 point deducted for violent conduct during match v. Arsenal.

APPENDIX 2
TOP SCORERS,
SEASON BY SEASON

	League		All Competitions	
1892–93	Bob Donaldson	16	Bob Donaldson	16
1893–94	Alf Farman	8	Bob Donaldson	10
1894–95	Dick Smith	19	Dick Smith	20
1895–96	Joe Cassidy	16	Joe Cassidy	16
1896–97	Joe Cassidy	17	Joe Cassidy	25
1897–98	Henry Boyd	22	Henry Boyd	22
1898–99	Joe Cassidy	19	Joe Cassidy	20
1899–1900	Joe Cassidy	16	Joe Cassidy	16
1900–01	William Jackson	14	William Jackson	15
1901–02	Steve Preston	11	Steve Preston	11
1902–03	Jack Peddie	11	Jack Peddie	15
1903–04	Billy Griffiths	11	Tommy Arkesden	15
	Tommy Arkesden	11		
	Billy Grassam	11		
1904–05	Jack Peddie	17	Jack Peddie	17
1905–06	Jack Picken	20	Jack Picken	25
1906–07	George Wall	11	George Wall	13
1907–08	Sandy Turnbull	25	Sandy Turnbull	27
1908–09	Jimmy Turnbull	17	Jimmy Turnbull	25
1909–10	George Wall	14	George Wall	14
1910–11	Enoch West	19	Enoch West	20
1911–12	Enoch West	17	Enoch West	23

	League		All Competitions	
1912–13	Enoch West	21	Enoch West	22
1913–14	George Anderson	15	George Anderson	15
1914–15	George Anderson	10	George Anderson	10
1915–19	No Competition			
1919–20	Joe Spence	14	Joe Spence	14
1920–21	Tom Miller	7	Tom Miller	8
	Teddy Partridge	7	Teddy Partridge	8
	George Sapsford	7		
	Joe Spence	7		
1921–22	Joe Spence	15	Joe Spence	15
1922–23	Ernie Goldthorpe	13	Ernie Goldthorpe	14
	Arthur Lochhead	13		
1923–24	Arthur Lochhead	14	Arthur Lochhead	14
1924–25	William Henderson	14	William Henderson	14
1925–26	Charlie Rennox	17	Frank McPherson	20
1926–27	Joe Spence	18	Joe Spence	19
1927–28	Joe Spence	22	Joe Spence	24
1928–29	Jimmy Hanson	19	Jimmy Hanson	20
1929–30	Joe Spence	12	Joe Spence	12
	Harry Rowley	12	Harry Rowley	12
1930–31	Tommy Reid	17	Tommy Reid	20
1931–32	Joe Spence	19	Joe Spence	19
1932–33	Bill Ridding	11	Bill Ridding	11
1933–34	Neil Dewar	8	Neil Dewar	8
1934–35	George Mutch	18	George Mutch	20
1935–36	George Mutch	21	George Mutch	23
1936–37	Tommy Bamford	14	Tommy Bamford	15
1937–38	Tommy Bamford	14	Tommy Barnford	15
			Harry Baird	15
1938–39	Jimmy Hanlon	12	Jimmy Hanlon	12
1939–46	No Competition			
1946–47	Jack Rowley	26	Jack Rowley	28

	League		All Competitions	
1947–48	Jack Rowley	23	Jack Rowley	28
1948–49	Jack Rowley	20	Jack Rowley	30
1949–50	Jack Rowley	20	Jack Rowley	23
1950–51	Stan Pearson	18	Stan Pearson	23
1951–52	Jack Rowley	30	Jack Rowley	30
1952–53	Stan Pearson	16	Stan Pearson	18
1953–54	Tommy Taylor	22	Tommy Tayfor	23
1954–55	Dennis Viollet	20	Dennis Viollet	21
	Tommy Taylor	20		
1955–56	Tommy Taylor	25	Tommy Taylor	25
1956–57	Billy Whelan	26	Tommy Taylor	34
1957–58	Dennis Viollet	16	Dennis Viollet	23
	Tommy Taylor	16		
1958–59	Bobby Charlton	29	Bobby Charlton	29
1959–60	Dennis Viollet	32	Dennis Viollet	32
1960–61	Bobby Charlton	21	Bobby Charlton	21
1961–62	David Herd	14	David Herd	17
1962–63	Denis Law	23	Denis Law	29
1963–64	Denis Law	30	Denis Law	46
1964–65	Denis Law	28	Denis Law	39
1965–66	David Herd	24	David Herd	33
1966–67	Denis Law	28	Denis Law	30
1967–68	George Best	28	George Best	32
1968–69	George Best	19	Denis Law	30
1969–70	George Best	15	George Best	23
1970–71	George Best	18	George Best	21
1971–72	George Best	18	George Best	26
1972–73	Bobby Charlton	6	Bobby Charlton	7
1973–74	Sammy McIlroy	6	Sammy McIlroy	6
			Lou Macari	6
1974–75	Stuart Pearson	17	Stuart Pearson	18
			Lou Macari	18

	League		All Competitions	
1975–76	Lou Macari	13	Lou Macari	16
	Stuart Pearson	13		
1976–77	Gordon Hill	15	Gordon Hill	20
	Stuart Pearson	15		
1977–78	Gordon Hill	17	Gordon Hill	19
1978–79	Jimmy Greenhoff	11	Jimmy Greenhoff	17
	Steve Coppell	11		
1979–80	Joe Jordan	13	Joe Jordan	13
1980–81	Joe Jordan	15	Joe Jordan	15
1981–82	Frank Stapleton	13	Frank Stapleton	13
1982–83	Frank Stapleton	14	Frank Stapleton	19
1983–84	Frank Stapleton	13	Frank Stapleton	19
1984–85	Mark Hughes	16	Mark Hughes	25
1985–86	Mark Hughes	17	Mark Hughes	18
1986–87	Peter Davenport	14	Peter Davenport	16
1987–88	Brian McClair	24	Brian McClair	31
1988–89	Mark Hughes	14	Mark Hughes	16
1989–90	Mark Hughes	13	Mark Hughes	15
1990–91	Brian McClair	13	Brian McClair	21
	Steve Bruce	13	Mark Hughes	21
1991–92	Brian McClair	18	Brian McClair	25
1992–93	Mark Hughes	15	Mark Hughes	16
1993–94	Eric Cantona	18	Eric Cantona	25
1994–95	Andrei Kancheiskis	14	Andrei Kanchelskis	15
1995–96	Eric Cantona	14	Eric Cantona	19
1996–97	Ole Gunnar Solskjaer	18	Ole Gunnar Solskjaer	19
1997–98	Andy Cole	15	Andy Cole	25
1998–99	Dwight Yorke	18	Dwight Yorke	29

APPENDIX 3
DEBUT GOALS

In all, 87 players have scored in their first appearance for Manchester United. Debut scores of two or more goals are noted in brackets. This list is based on the first match someone played in (including substitutions), rather than the first full appearance.

Jack Doughty	30 Oct. 1886	v. Fleetwood Rangers (FAC) (a)
T. Craig	18 Jan. 1890	v. Preston North End (FAC) (a)
George Evans	4 Oct. 1890	v. Higher Walton (FAC) (h)
J. Sneddon	3 Oct. 1891	v. Ardwick (FAC) (h)
Jimmy Coupar	3 Sept. 1892	v. Blackburn Rovers (a)
Bob Donaldson	3 Sept. 1892	v. Blackburn Rovers (a)
James Hendry	15 Oct. 1892	v. Wolves (h)
Tommy Fitzsimmons	19 Nov. 1892	v. Aston Villa (h)
George Millar	22 Dec.1894	v. Lincoln City (h)
John Aitken	7 Sept. 1895	v. Crewe Alexandra (h)
William Kennedy	7 Sept. 1895	v. Crewe Alexandra (h)
Jimmy Collinson	16 Nov. 1895	v. Lincoln City (h)
R. Stephenson	11 Jan. 1896	v. Rotherham Town (h)
Henry Boyd	20 Jan. 1897	v. Blackpool (FAC) (a)
	(and on League debut)	
Frank Wedge	20 Nov. 1897	v. Leicester Fosse (a)
William Brooks (2)	22 Oct. 1898	v. Loughborough Town (h)
Jimmy Bain	16 Sept. 1899	v. Loughborough Town (h)
Tom Leigh	17 Mar. 1900	v. Barnsley (h)
Edward Holt	28 Apr. 1900	v. Chesterfield (h)

John Grundy	28 Apr. 1900	v. Chesterfield (h)
Steve Preston	7 Sept. 1901	v. Gainsborough Trinity (h)
Billy Richards	21 Dec. 1901	v. Burslem Port Vale (h)
Charlie Richards	6 Sept. 1902	v. Gainsborough Trinity (h)
Arthur Beadsworth	25 Oct. 1902	v. Woolwich Arsenal (a) (and on FAC debut)
Alex Downie	22 Nov. 1902	v. Leicester Fosse (a)
John Fitchett	21 Mar. 1903	v. Leicester Fosse (h)
Dick Duckworth	19 Dec.1903	v. Gainsborough Trinity (h)
Jack Allan (2)	3 Sept. 1904	v. Burslem Port Vale (a) (and on FAC debut)
Harry Williams	10 Sept. 1904	v. Bristol City (h)
Jack Picken	2 Sept. 1905	v. Bristol City (h) (and on FAC debut)
Charlie Sagar (3)	2 Sept. 1905	v. Bristol City (h) (and on FAC debut)
George Wall	7 Apr. 1906	v. Clapton Orient (a) (and on FAC debut)
Alex Menzies	17 Nov. 1906	v. The Wednesday (a)
Sandy Turnbull	1 Jan. 1907	v. Aston Villa (h)
Joe Williams	25 Mar. 1907	v. Sunderland (h)
Harold Halse	28 Mar. 1908	v. The Wednesday (h) (and on FAC debut)
George Livingstone (2)	23 Jan. 1909	v. Manchester City (h)
Arthur Hooper	22 Jan. 1910	v. Tottenham Hotspur (h)
Enoch West	1 Sept. 1910	v. Woolwich Arsenal (a) (and on FAC debut)
Tom Nuttall	23 Mar. 1912	v. Liverpool (h)
Frank Harris	14 Feb. 1920	v. Sunderland (h)
Harry Leonard	11 Sept. 1920	v. Chelsea (h)
William Henderson	26 Nov. 1921	v. Aston Villa (h)
John Wood	26 Aug. 1922	v. Crystal Palace (h)
Jimmy Hanson	15 Nov. 1924	v. Hull City (h)

Albert Pape	7 Feb. 1925	v. Clapton Orient (h)
Eric Sweeney	13 Feb. 1926	v. Leeds United (h)
George Nicol (2)	11 Feb. 1928	v. Leicester City (h)
Bill Rawlings	14 Mar. 1928	v. Everton (h)
Tommy Reid (2)	2 Feb. 1929	v. West Ham United (h)
	(and on FAC debut)	
John Ball	11 Sept. 1929	v. Leicester City (h)
Arthur Warburton	8 Mar. 1930	v. Aston Villa (h)
Arthur Fitton	26 Mar. 1932	v. Oldham Athletic (h)
James Brown	17 Sept. 1932	v. Grimsby Town (h)
Neil Dewar	11 Feb. 1933	v. Preston North End (a)
David Byrne	21 Oct. 1933	v. Bury (a)
Bill Owen	22 Sept. 1934	v. Norwich City (h)
Tommy Bamford	20 Oct. 1934	v. Newcastle United (a)
	(and on FAC debut)	
Ernie Thompson	21 Nov. 1936	v. Liverpool (h)
Reg Halton	12 Dec. 1936	v. Middlesbrough (a)
George Gladwin	27 Feb. 1937	v. Chelsea (a)
Jack Smith	2 Feb. 1938	v. Barnsley (a)
Jimmy Hanlon	26 Nov. 1938	v. Huddersfield Town (h)
Len Bradbury	28 Jan. 1939	v. Chelsea (a)
Bill Bainbridge	9 Jan. 1946	v. Accrington Stanley (FAC) (h)
Charlie Mitten	31 Aug. 1946	v. Grimsby Town (h)
Ted Buckle	4 Jan. 1947	v. Charlton Athletic (h)
	(and on FAC debut)	
John Downie	5 Mar. 1949	v. Charlton Athletic (a)
	(and on FAC debut)	
Eddie Lewis	29 Nov. 1952	v. West Bromwich Albion (a)
Tommy Taylor (2)	7 Mar. 1953	v. Preston North End (h)
Bobby Charlton (2)	6 Oct. 1956	v. Charlton Athletic (h)
	(and on FAC debut)	
Alex Dawson	22 Apr. 1957	v. Burnley (h)
	(and on FAC and LC debuts)	
Shay Brennan (2)	19 Feb. 1958	v. Sheffield Wednesday (FAC) (h)

Denis Law	18 Aug. 1962 v. West Bromwich Albion (h)
	(and on FAC, ECC and ICFC debuts)
Albert Kinsey	9 Jan. 1965 v. Chester (FAC) (h)
Alan Gowling	30 Mar. 1968 v. Stoke City (a)
Sammy McIlroy	6 Nov. 1971 v. Manchester City (a)
Ian Storey-Moore	11 Mar. 1972 v. Huddersfield Town (h)
Wyn Davies	23 Sept. 1972 v. Derby County (h)
Lou Macari	20 Jan. 1973 v. West Ham United (h)
	(and on FAC debut)
Gordon Strachan	25 Aug. 1984 v. Watford (h)
	(and on FAC debut)
Peter Barnes	31 Aug. 1985 v. Nottingham Forest (a)
	(and on LC debut)
Neil Webb	19 Aug. 1989 v. Arsenal (h)
	(and on FAC, LC and ECWC debuts)
Danny Wallace	20 Sept. 1989 v. Portsmouth (LC) (a)
Keith Gillespie	5 Jan. 1993 v. Bury (FAC) (h)
Paul Scholes (2)	21 Sept. 1994 v. Port Vale (LC) (a)
	(and on League debut)
Ole Gunnar Solskjaer	25 Aug. 1996 v. Blackburn Rovers (h)
	(and on LC debut)

APPENDIX 4
ALL-TIME HAT-TRICK LIST

United players have scored 191 hat-tricks for the club. (D indicates a double hat-trick; tallies of four or more goals are noted in brackets.)

15 Oct. 1892 D	Bob Donaldson	v. Wolves (h)
	Willie Stewart	v. Wolves (h)
31 Dec. 1892 D	Bob Donaldson	v. Derby County (h)
	Alf Farman	v. Derby County (h)
27 Apr. 1893	Alf Farman	v. Small Heath (test match) (n)
2 Sept. 1893	Alf Farman	v. Burnley (h)
12 Mar. 1894	Bob Donaldson	v. Blackburn Rovers (h)
3 Nov. 1894	Dick Smith (4)	v. Manchester City (a)
2 Nov. 1895	James Peters	v. Liverpool (h)
1 Jan. 1896	Joe Cassidy	v. Grimsby Town (h)
3 Apr. 1896	William Kennedy	v. Darwen (h)
26 Sept. 1896	Joe Cassidy	v. Newcastle United (h)
24 Oct. 1896	Joe Cassidy	v. Burton Wanderers (h)
30 Jan. 1897	Joe Cassidy	v. Kettering Town (FAC) (h)
1 Apr. 1897	Caesar Jenkyns	v. Lincoln City (a)
4 Sept. 1897	Henry Boyd	v. Lincoln City (h)
11 Sept. 1897	Henry Boyd	v. Burton Swifts (a)
29 Mar. 1898	Henry Boyd	v. Loughborough Town (h)
24 Dec. 1898 D	William Bryant	v. Darwen (h)
	Joe Cassidy	v. Darwen (h)
1 Feb. 1899	William Bryant	v. Tottenham Hotspur (FAC) (h)
20 Jan. 1900	Matthew Gillespie	v. Burton Swifts (h)

31 Mar. 1900	Joe Cassidy	v. Luton Town (h)
26 Oct. 1901	Jimmy Coupar	v. Doncaster Rovers (h)
1 Nov. 1902	Fred Williams	v. Accrington Stanley (FAC) (h)
29 Nov. 1902	Dick Pegg	v. Southport Central (FAC) (h)
26 Sept. 1903	Dick Pegg	v. Bradford City (h)
17 Dec. 1904	Jack Peddie	v. Burton United (a)
31 Dec. 1904	Jack Allan	v. Burslem Port Vale (h)
18 Feb. 1905	Jack Peddie	v. Leicester Fosse (h)
1 Apr. 1905	Dick Duckworth	v. Doncaster Rovers (h)
2 Sept. 1905	Charlie Sagar	v. Bristol City (h)
6 Jan. 1906	Clem Beddow	v. Grimsby Town (h)
13 Jan. 1906	Clem Beddow	v. Staple Hill (FAC) (h)
24 Feb. 1906	Jack Picken	v. Aston Villa (FAC) (h)
17 Mar. 1906	Jack Picken	v. Chesterfield (h)
29 Mar. 1906	Jack Peddie	v. Leicester Fosse (a)
31 Mar. 1906	Charlie Sagar	v. Barnsley (h)
10 Apr. 1907	George Wall	v. The Wednesday (h)
7 Sept. 1907	Sandy Turnbull	v. Liverpool (h)
19 Oct. 1907	Sandy Turnbull	v. Blackburn Rovers (a)
23 Nov. 1907	Sandy Turnbull (4)	v. Woolwich Arsenal (h)
29 Aug. 1908	Jimmy Turnbull	v. Queen's Park Rangers (CS) (n)
12 Sept. 1908	Jimmy Turnbull (4)	v. Middlesbrough (h)
12 Dec. 1908	George Wall	v. Leicester Fosse (h)
20 Feb. 1909 D	Sandy Turnbull	v. Blackburn Rovers (FAC) (h)
	Jimmy Turnbull	v. Blackburn Rovers (FAC) (h)
30 Apr. 1910	Jack Picken (4)	v. Middlesbrough (h)
25 Sept. 1911	Harold Halse (6)	v. Swindon Town (CS) (n)
14 Dec. 1912	Enoch West	v. Newcastle United (a)
18 Oct. 1913	George Anderson	v. Preston North End (h)
29 Oct. 1921	Joe Spence	v. Manchester City (h)
10 Feb. 1923	Ernie Goldthorpe (4)	v. Notts County (a)
22 Dec. 1923	Jimmy Bain	v. Port Vale (h)
12 Apr. 1924	Joe Spence (4)	v. Crystal Palace (h)
20 Sept. 1924	William Henderson	v. Oldham Athletic (a)

Date	Player	Opponent
26 Sept. 1925	Charlie Rennox	v. Burnley (h)
28 Dec. 1925	Frank McPherson	v. Leicester City (a)
21 Apr. 1926	Chris Taylor	v. Sunderland (h)
1 May 1926	Chris Taylor	v. West Bromwich Albion (h)
22 Oct. 1927	Joe Spence	v. Derby County (h)
14 Jan. 1928	Jimmy Hanson (4)	v. Brentford (FAC) (h)
7 Apr. 1928	Bill Rawlings	v. Burnley (h)
5 May 1928	Joe Spence	v. Liverpool (h)
14 Sept. 1929	Bill Rawlings	v. Middlesbrough (a)
1 Feb. 1930	Joe Spence (4)	v. West Ham United (h)
13 Sept. 1930	Tommy Reid	v. Newcastle United (h)
8 Nov. 1930	Jimmy Bullock	v. Leicester City (a)
10 Jan. 1931	Tommy Reid	v. Stoke City (FAC) (a)
30 Jan. 1932	Tommy Reid	v. Nottingham Forest (h)
26 Mar. 1932	Tommy Reid	v. Oldham Athletic (h)
22 Oct. 1932	Tommy Reid	v. Millwall (h)
17 Dec.1932	Tommy Reid	v. Lincoln City (h)
23 Sept. 1933	Neil Dewar (4)	v. Burnley (h)
8 Sept. 1934	George Mutch	v. Barnsley (h)
30 Mar. 1935	Billy Boyd	v. Hull City (h)
23 Nov. 1934	Harry Rowley	v. Norwich City (a)
8 Feb. 1936	Tom Manley (4)	v. Port Vale (h)
5 Sept. 1936	Tommy Bamford	v. Derby County (a)
11 Sept. 1937	Tommy Bamford	v. Barnsley (h)
13 Nov. 1937	Tommy Bamford (4)	v. Chesterfield (a)
4 Dec. 1937	Jack Rowley (4)	v. Swansea Town (h)
18 Feb. 1939	Jimmy Hanlon	v. Blackpool (a)
11 Sept. 1946	Stan Pearson	v. Liverpool (h)
7 Dec. 1946	Jack Rowley	v. Brentford (h)
26 May 1947	Jack Rowley	v. Sheffield United (h)
30 Aug. 1947	Jack Rowley (4)	v. Charlton Athletic (h)
8 Nov. 1947	Jack Rowley (4)	v. Huddersfield Town (h)
29 Nov. 1947	Johnny Morris	v. Chelsea (a)
1 Jan. 1948	Jack Rowley	v. Burnley (h)

13 Mar. 1948	Stan Pearson	v. Derby County (FAC) (n)
1 May 1948	Stan Pearson	v. Blackburn Rovers (h)
27 Nov. 1948	Jack Rowley	v. Middlesbrough (a)
12 Feb. 1949	Jack Rowley (5)	v. Yeovil Town (FAC) (h)
8 Mar. 1950	Charlie Mitten (4)	v. Aston Villa (h)
27 Jan. 1951	Stan Pearson	v. Leeds United (FAC) (h)
31 Mar. 1951	Stan Pearson	v. Chelsea (h)
18 Aug. 1951	Jack Rowley	v. West Bromwich Albion (a)
22 Aug. 1951	Jack Rowley	v. Middlesbrough (h)
8 Sept. 1951	Jack Rowley	v. Stoke City (h)
26 Apr. 1952	Jack Rowley	v. Arsenal (h)
10 Sept. 1952	Stan Pearson	v. Derby County (a)
21 Nov. 1953	Tommy Taylor	v. Blackpool (h)
25 Dec. 1953	Tommy Taylor	v. Sheffield Wednesday (h)
9 Oct. 1954	Tommy Taylor (4)	v. Cardiff City (h)
16 Oct. 1954	Dennis Viollet	v. Chelsea (a)
11 Dec. 1954	Colin Webster	v. Burnley (a)
24 Dec. 1955	Dennis Viollet	v. West Bromwich Albion (a)
29 Aug. 1956	Dennis Viollet	v. Preston North End (h)
26 Sept. 1956 D	Dennis Viollet (4)	v. Anderlecht (ECC) (h)
	Tommy Taylor	v. Anderlecht (ECC) (h)
18 Feb. 1957	Bobby Charlton	v. Charlton Athletic (a)
19 Apr. 1957	Billy Whelan	v. Burnley (a)
24 Aug. 1957	Billy Whelan	v. Leicester City (a)
22 Oct. 1957	Tommy Taylor	v. Aston Villa (CS) (h)
4 Jan. 1958	Dennis Viollet	v. Workington (FAC) (a)
18 Jan. 1958	Bobby Charlton	v. Bolton Wanderers (h)
26 Mar. 1958	Alex Dawson	v. Fulham (FAC) (n)
23 Aug. 1958	Bobby Charlton	v. Chelsea (h)
17 Sept. 1958	Albert Scanion	v. West Ham United (h)
21 Mar. 1959	Dennis Viollet	v. Leeds United (h)
12 Dec. 1959	Dennis Viollet	v. Nottingham Forest (a)
27 Feb. 1960	Bobby Charlton	v. Blackpool (a)
30 Apr. 1960	Alex Dawson	v. Everton (h)

15 Oct. 1960	Dennis Viollet	v. Burnley (a)
26 Dec. 1960	Alex Dawson	v. Chelsea (h)
31 Dec. 1960	Alex Dawson	v. Manchester City (h)
12 Apr. 1961 D	Dennis Viollet	v. Burnley (h)
	Albert Quixall	v. Burnley (h)
26 Dec. 1961	Nobby Lawton	v. Nottingham Forest (h)
7 Apr. 1962	Albert Quixall	v. Ipswich Town (h)
3 Nov. 1962	Denis Law (4)	v. Ipswich Town (a)
4 Mar. 1963	Denis Law	v. Huddersfield Town (FAC) (h)
16 Apr. 1963	Denis Law	v. Leicester City (a)
3 Sept. 1963	Denis Law	v. Ipswich Town (a)
15 Oct. 1963	Denis Law	v. Willem II Tilburg (ECWC) (h)
9 Nov. 1963	Denis Law	v. Tottenham Hotspur (h)
7 Dec. 1963	Denis Law (4)	v. Stoke City (h)
14 Dec. 1963	David Herd	v. Sheffield Wednesday (h)
25 Jan. 1964	Denis Law	v. Bristol Rovers (FAC) (h)
26 Feb. 1964	Denis Law	v. Sporting Lisbon (ECWC) (h)
9 Mar. 1964	Denis Law	v. Sunderland (FAC) (n)
24 Oct. 1964	Denis Law (4)	v. Aston Villa (h)
27 Oct. 1964	Denis Law	v. Djurgårdens (ICFC) (h)
11 Nov. 1964	Bobby Charlton	v. Borussia Dortmund (ICFC) (a)
3 Apr. 1965	Bobby Charlton	v. Blackburn Rovers (a)
18 Sept. 1965	Denis Law	v. Chelsea (h)
6 Oct. 1965	John Connelly	v. HJK Helsinki (ECC) (h)
23 Oct. 1965	David Herd	v. Fulham (h)
1 Dec. 1965	David Herd	v. ASK Vorwärts (ECC) (h)
5 Feb. 1966	Bobby Charlton	v. Northampton Town (h)
26 Feb. 1966	David Herd	v. Burnley (h)
26 Nov. 1966	David Herd (4)	v. Sunderland (h)
17 Dec. 1966	David Herd	v. West Bromwich Albion (a)
4 May 1968	George Best	v. Newcastle United (h)
18 Sept. 1968	Denis Law	v. Waterford (ECC) (a)
2 Oct. 1968	Denis Law (4)	v. Waterford (ECC) (h)
18 Jan. 1969	Denis Law	v. Sunderland (h)

24 Feb. 1969	Denis Law	v. Birmingham City (FAC) (h)
19 Mar. 1969	Willie Morgan	V. Queen's Park Rangers (h)
7 Feb. 1970	George Best (6)	v. Northampton Town (FAC) (a)
20 Feb. 1971	Alan Gowling (4)	v. Southampton (h)
17 Apr. 1971	Denis Law	v. Crystal Palace (a)
18 Sept. 1971	George Best	v. West Ham United (h)
27 Nov. 1971	George Best	v. Southampton (a)
24 Aug. 1974	Gerry Daly	v. Millwall (h)
2 Nov. 1974	Stuart Pearson	v. Oxford United (h)
27 Oct. 1976	Gordon Hill	v. Newcastle United (LC) (h)
19 Feb. 1977	Jimmy Greenhoff	v. Newcastle United (h)
20 Aug. 1977	Lou Macari	v. Birmingham City (a)
24 Mar. 1979	Andy Ritchie	v. Leeds United (h)
12 Apr. 1980	Andy Ritchie	v. Tottenham Hotspur (h)
3 Oct. 1981	Sammy McIlroy	v. Wolves (h)
19 Nov. 1983	Frank Stapleton	v. Watford (h)
26 Sept. 1984	Mark Hughes	v. Burnley (LC) (h)
9 Mar. 1985	Norman Whiteside	v. West Ham United (FAC) (h)
23 Mar. 1985	Mark Hughes	v. Aston Villa (h)
22 Feb. 1986	Jesper Olsen	v. West Bromwich Albion (h)
2 Apr.1988	Brian McClair	v. Derby County (h)
12 Oct. 1988	Brian McClair	v. Rotherham United (LC) (h)
16 Sept. 1989	Mark Hughes	v. Millwall (h)
28 Nov. 1990	Lee Sharpe	v. Arsenal (LC) (a)
23 Jan. 1991	Mark Hughes	v. Southampton (LC) (h)
10 Nov. 1994	Andrei Kanchelskis	v. Manchester City (h)
4 Mar. 1995	Andy Cole (5)	v. Ipswich Town (h)
25 Oct. 1997	Andy Cole	v. Barnsley (h)
5 Nov. 1997	Andy Cole	v. Feyenoord (ECC) (a)
16 Jan. 1999	Dwight Yorke	v. Leicester City (a)
6 Feb. 1999	Ole Gunnar Solskjaer (4)	v. Nottingham Forest (a)

APPENDIX 5
GOALKEEPER PERFORMANCE

United have used 77 goalkeepers over the past 113 years. Their relative performances in terms of goals conceded per game are as follows:

		Games	Goals	Average
T. Beckett	1886	1	2	2.00
Tom Hay	1890	1	6	6.00
William Gyves	1890	1	1	1.00
J. Slater	1890–91	4	5	1.25
Jimmy Warner	1892–93	22	58	2.64
John Davies	1893	10	26	2.60
Willie Stewart	1890–94	1	7	7.00*
Joe Fall	1893–94	27	59	2.19
William Douglas	1894–96	57	104	1.82
Joe Ridgway	1896–98	17	24	1.41
George Perrins	1892–95	2	7	3.50*
Walter Whittaker	1895	3	9	3.00
Walter Cartwright	1896–1903	2	4	2.00*
Joe Wetherell	1896	2	3	1.50
Frank Barrett	1896–1900	136	148	1.09[1]
James Garvey	1900–01	6	6	1.00
Jimmy Whitehouse	1900–03	63	90	1.43
James Saunders	1901–02	13	16	1.23
Herbert Birchenough	1902–03	30	33	1.10
John Sutcliffe	1903–04	28	36	1.29

		Games	Goals	Average
Harry Moger	1903–12	266	328	1.23[2]
Bob Valentine	1905–06	10	8	0.80
Archie Montgomery	1905	3	2	0.66
Herbert Broomfield	1908	9	11	1.22
Tom Wilcox	1908–09	2	4	2.00
Elijah Round	1909–10	2	10	5.00
Hugh Edmonds	1911–12	51	70	1.37[2]
Ezra Royals	1912–14	7	14	2.00
Robert Beale	1912–15	112	156	1.39
Jack Mew (Eng)	1913–26	199	282	1.42
Alf Steward	1921–32	326	525	1.61
Lance Richardson	1926–28	42	82	1.95
Arthur Chesters	1929–31	9	30	3.33
John Moody	1932–33	51	78	1.53
Charlie Hillam	1933–34	8	21	2.63
Jack Hall	1933–36	73	108	1.48
Billy Behan	1934	1	1	1.00
Jack Hacking	1934–35	34	40	1.18
Len Langford	1934–35	15	22	1.47
Jack Breedon	1935–39	38	52	1.37[3]
Roy John	1936	15	36	2.40
Tommy Breen (NI)	1936–39	71	93	1.31
Norman Tapken	1938–39	16	32	2.00
Jack Crompton	1945–55	211	249	1.18[2]
Cliff Collinson	1946	7	11	1.57
Bill Fielding	1947	7	15	2.14
Ken Pegg	1947	2	3	1.50
Berry Brown	1948	4	5	1.25
Sonny Feehan	1949–50	14	16	1.14
Ray Wood (Eng)	1949–58	208	292	1.40[2]
Joe Lancaster	1950	4	5	1.25
Reg Allen	1950–52	80	92	1.15

		Games	Goals	Average
Johnny Carey (Ire)	1953	1	2	2.00*
Les Olive	1953	2	3	1.50
David Gaskell	1956–66	120	210	1.75[2]
Tony Hawksworth	1956	1	2	2.00
Gordon Clayton	1957	2	2	1.00
Harry Gregg (NI)	1957–66	247	394	1.60
Ronnie Briggs (NI)	1960–62	11	24	2.18
Mike Pinner	1961	4	5	1.25
Pat Dunne (Ire)	1964–65	66	67	1.02
Alex Stepney (Eng)	1966–78	539	632	1.17[2, 4]
Jimmy Rimmer	1968–73	46	67	1.46
John Connaughton	1972	3	6	2.00
Paddy Roche (Ire)	1975–81	53	89	1.68
Gary Bailey (Eng)	1978–87	375	339	0.90[2]
Jeff Wealands	1983	8	11	1.37
Stephen Pears	1985	5	4	0.80
Chris Turner	1985–88	79	76	0.96
Gary Walsh	1986–95	63	71	1.13
Jim Leighton (Sco)	1988–90	94	102	1.09
Les Sealey	1990–94	56	56	1.00[2]
Mark Bosnich (Aust)	1990–	3	2	0.66
Peter Schmeichel (Den)	1991–99	398	328	0.82[2, 5]
Ian Wilkinson	1991	1	1	1.00
Kevin Pilkington	1994–97	8	13	1.62
Raimond van der Gouw	1996–	20	17	0.85

* Outfielder.

1 Includes four test matches in 1897.

2 Includes Charity Shield.

3 Includes three matches in the abandoned 1939–40 season.

4 Includes World Club Championship.
5 Includes 1991 European Super Cup.

⟨⟩ Peter Schmeichel, with an average of 0.82 goals conceded per game, has the best average of any goalkeeper to have played more than ten games. His nearest challengers are Raimond van der Gouw (0.85) and Gary Bailey (0.90).

⟨⟩ The keepers with the worst averages over more than ten games are Jimmy Warner on 2.64, John Davies on 2.60 and Roy John on 2.40. Arthur Chesters' 30 goals conceded escapes inclusion because he only played nine games, but even had he played a tenth match and kept a clean sheet, his average would still be an appalling 3.00. The worst postwar average is Ronnie Briggs's 2.18.

⟨⟩ The most appearances by United goalkeepers to the summer of 1999 are:

		Dates	Games	Goals	Average
1	Alex Stepney (Eng)	1966–78	539	632	1.17
2	Peter Schmeichel (Den)	1991–99	398	328	0.82
3	Gary Bailey (Eng)	1978–87	375	339	0.90
4	Alf Steward	1921–32	326	525	1.61
5	Harry Moger	1903–12	266	328	1.23
6	Harry Gregg (NI)	1957–66	247	394	1.60
7	Jack Crompton	1945–55	211	249	1.18
8	Ray Wood (Eng)	1949–58	208	292	1.40
9	Jack Mew (Eng)	1913–26	199	282	1.42
10	Frank Barrett	1896–1900	136	148	1.09

APPENDIX 6
PENALTY TOTALS, SEASON BY SEASON

The following table lists United's penalties, scored and missed, in each season since the war. It excludes penalty shoot-outs:

		Scored	Missed
1946–47	4	Buckle 2, Wrigglesworth 1, Rowley 1	Wrigglesworth 1, Buckle 1
1947–48	3	Mitten 2, Buckle 1	Rowley 1
1948–49	7	Mitten 7	Mitten 1
1949–50	7	Mitten 7	Mitten 3
1950–51	1	Rowley 1	Rowley 3, McShane 1
1951–52	2	Rowley 1, Byrne 1	Byrne 1, Rowley 1
1952–53	5	Byrne 3, Rowley 2	Byrne 1
1953–54	3	Byrne 3	T. Taylor 1
1954–55	2	Byrne 2	–
1955–56	4	Byrne 3, Berry 1	Byrne 2
1956–57	5	Berry 3, Byrne 1, Scanlon 1	Berry 3
1957–58	4	Edwards 2, E.Taylor 1, Berry 1*	Berry 2
1958–59	7	Charlton 6, Quixall 1	Charlton 2
1959–60	3	Quixall 3	–
1960–61	7	Quixall 6, Cantwell 1	Quixall 1, Viollet 1
1961–62	4	Quixall 3, Brennan 1	Quixall 1, Cantwell 1
1962–63	5	Quixall 5	Quixall 2, Brennan 1, Charlton 1

		Scored	Missed
1963–64	4	Law 4	Law 1
1964–65	3	Law 2, Charlton 1	–
1965–66	2	Law 2	–
1966–67	3	Law 2, Best 1	Law 1
1967–68	4	Law 2, Best 2	Law 2, Best 1, Charlton 1
1968–69	4	Law 3, Best 1	Law 3
1969–70	4	Morgan 3, Best 1	–
1970–71	3	Morgan 2, Best 1	Morgan 1
1971–72	5	Morgan 3, Best 2	–
1972–73	5	Best 3, Charlton 2	Best 1
1973–74	3	Stepney 2, McCalliog 1	Stepney 1
1974–75	10	Daly 9, McCalliog 1	–
1975–76	4	Daly 4	–
1976–77	6	Daly 3, Hill 2, J.Greenhoff 1	Daly 1, McIlroy 1
1977–78	9	Hill 7, Pearson 1, Grimes 1	Hill 1, B.Greenhoff 1, Pearson 1
1978–79	2	J.Greenhoff 2	J. Greenhoff 1, McQueen 1
1979–80	4	McIlroy 3, Thomas 1	Thomas 1, Grimes 1
1980–81	3	McIlroy 3	–
1981–82	2	Coppell 1, Stapleton 1	Gidman 1, Stapleton 1
1982–83	4	Coppell 2, Grimes 1, Muhren 1	–
1983–84	7	Muhren 4, Wilkins 3	Muhren 1, Wilkins 1
1984–85	11	Strachan 9, Muhren 1, Whiteside 1	Strachan 5, Whiteside 1
1985–86	9	Olsen 5, Robson 2, Strachan 1, Davenport 1	Robson 1, Whiteside 1
1986–87	6	Davenport 5, Olsen 1	Olsen 1, Robson 2, Strachan 1
1987–88	6	McClair 6	McClair 3, Davenport 1, Olsen 1

		Scored	Missed
1988–89	1	McClair 1	McClair 1
1989–90	1	Bruce 1	McClair 1
1990–91	12	Bruce 11, Blackmore 1	Bruce 1
1991–92	4	Bruce 3, Blackmore 1	Bruce 2
1992–93	3	Bruce 2, Cantona 1	Bruce 1
1993–94	4	Cantona 4	–
1994–95	7	Cantona 5*, Irwin 2	Butt 1
1995–96	5	Cantona 5	–
1996–97	3	Cantona 3	Cantona 2, Scholes 1
1997–98	3	Irwin 3	Sheringham 3
1998–99	2	Irwin 2	Yorke 1, Irwin 1

* includes penalty in Charity Shield

Total taken since 1945: 330. Scored: 241. Missed: 89. Success rate: 73 %.

APPENDIX 7
DISMISSALS

The following table lists many of the occasions when United players have been dismissed from the field of play. The list is very incomplete, especially for the pre-war period, though it is reasonably accurate since 1945.

21 Dec. 1907	Sandy Turnbull	v. Manchester City (h)
16 Jan. 1909	Billy Meredith	v. Brighton & Hove Albion (FAC) (h)
16 Oct. 1909	Jimmy Turnbull	v. Aston Villa (h)
23 Oct. 1909	Jimmy Turnbull	v. Sheffield United (a)
22 Apr. 1911	Enoch West	v. Aston Villa (a)
27 Aug. 1928	Jimmy Hanson	v. Aston Villa (a)
2 Sept. 1929	Charlie Moore	v. Leicester City (a)
29 Oct. 1932	Tommy Frame	v. Port Vale (a)
3 Sept. 1949	Henry Cockburn [with Linacre]	v. Manchester City (h)
29 May 1951	Brian Birch	v. Aalborg (fr) (a)
29 Jan. 1955	Allenby Chilton	v. Manchester City (FAC) (a)
15 Mar. 1958	Mark Pearson	v. Burnley (a)
1 Oct. 1958	Colin Webster	v. Young Boys Berne (fr) (h)
8 Aug. 1959	Albert Quixall	v. Bayern Munich (fr) (a)
8 Aug. 1959	Joe Carolan	v. Bayern Munich (fr) (a)
16 May 1962	Maurice Setters	v. Mallorca (fr) (a)
13 Aug. 1963	Noel Cantwell	v. Eintracht Frankfurt (fr) (a)
25 Sept. 1963	David Herd	v. Willem II (ECWC) (a)
16 Nov. 1963	Denis Law	v. Aston Villa (a)
26 Dec. 1963	Pat Crerand	v. Burnley (a)

14 Nov. 1964	Denis Law	v. Blackpool (a)
5 June 1965	Pat Crerand [with Orosz]	v. Ferencváros (a)
6 Nov. 1965	Harry Gregg	v. Blackburn Rovers (h)
19 Apr.1966	Pat Crerand [with Mihaslović]	v. Partizan Belgrade (h)
12 Aug. 1966	Nobby Stiles	v. F K Austria (fr) (a)
27 June 1967	Denis Law	v. Western Australia (fr) (a)
7 Oct. 1967	Denis Law	v. Arsenal (h) [with Ure]
13 Jan. 1968	Brian Kidd [with Kinnear]	v. Tottenham Hotspur (FAC) (a)
25 Sept. 1968	Nobby Stiles	v. Estudiantes (WCC) (a)
16 Oct. 1968	George Best [with Medina]	v. Estudiantes (WCC) (h)
23 Apr. 1969	John Fitzpatrick	v. A C Milan (ECC) (a)
1 May 1971	Pat Crerand [with Craven]	v. Blackpool (a)
18 Aug. 1971	George Best	v. Chelsea (a)
18 May 1972	Tony Young	v. Mallorca (fr) (a)
13 Jan. 1973	Tony Dunne	v. Wolves (FAC) (a)
4 Feb. 1973	Jim Holton	v. FC Porto (fr) (a)
17 Mar. 1973	Jim Holton	v. Newcastle United (h)
18 Aug. 1973	Lou Macari	v. Real Murcia (fr) (a)
13 Mar. 1974	Lou Macari [with Doyle]	v. Manchester City (a)
3 Aug. 1975	Jim Holton	v. Halskov (fr) (a)
7 Aug. 1975	Lou Macari	v. Holstebro (fr) (a)
7 May 1977	Sammy McIlroy	v. Bristol City (a)
7 Jan. 1978	Brian Greenhoff	v. Carlisle United (FAC) (a)
10 Aug. 1978	Joe Jordan	v. Holstebro (fr) (a)
30 Aug. 1978	Gordon McQueen	v. Stockport County (LC) (h)
1 Aug. 1979	Mickey Thomas	v. Bochum (fr) (a)
2 Apr. 1980	Sammy McIlroy	v. Nottingham Forest (a)
30 Oct. 1982	Ashley Grimes	v. West Ham United (a)

Date	Player	Match
2 May 1983	Remi Moses	v. Arsenal (a)
14 Aug. 1983	Gordon McQueen	v. Aiax (fr) (a)
24 Nov. 1984	Mark Hughes [with Hodgson]	v. Sunderland (a)
18 May 1985	Kevin Moran	v. Everton (FAC final) (W)
26 Oct. 1985	Graeme Hogg	v. Chelsea (a)
25 Jan. 1986	Bryan Robson	v. Sunderland (FAC) (a)
3 Jan. 1987	Liam O'Brien	v. Southampton (a)
4 Apr. 1988	Colin Gibson	v. Liverpool (a)
13 Jan. 1990	Steve Bruce	v. Derby County (h)
4 Sept. 1990	Steve Bruce	v. Luton Town (a)
6 Oct. 1991	Mark Hughes	v. Liverpool (h)
29 Sept. 1992	Mark Hughes	v. Torpedo Moscow (UEFA) (a)
25 July 1993	Bryan Robson	v. Arsenal (fr) (n)
3 Nov. 1993	Eric Cantona (after final whistle)	v. Galatasaray (ECC) (a)
9 Jan. 1994	Mark Hughes	v. Sheffield United (FAC) (a)
12 Mar. 1994	Peter Schmeichel	v. Charlton Athletic (FAC) (h)
19 Mar. 1994	Eric Cantona	v. Swindon Town (a)
22 Mar. 1994	Eric Cantona	v. Arsenal (a)
27 Mar. 1994	Andrei Kanchelskis	v. Aston Villa (LC final) (W)
6 Aug. 1994	Eric Cantona	v. Rangers (fr) (a)
20 Aug. 1994	Paul Parker	v. Queen's Park Rangers (h)
23 Nov. 1994	Paul Ince	v. Gothenburg (ECL) (a)
26 Nov. 1994	Mark Hughes	v. Arsenal (a)
25 Jan. 1995	Eric Cantona	v. Crystal Palace (a)
12 Apr. 1995	Roy Keane [with Patterson]	v. Crystal Palace (FAC) (n)
28 Aug. 1995	Roy Keane	v. Blackburn Rovers (a)
20 Sept. 1995	Pat McGibbon	v. York City (LC) (h)
28 Oct. 1995	Roy Keane	v. Middlesbrough (h)
22 Jan. 1996	Nicky Butt	v. West Ham United (a)
26 Oct. 1996	Roy Keane	v. Southampton (a)

20 Sept. 1997	Gary Pallister (later rescinded)	v. Bolton Wanderers (a) [with Blake]
18 Apr. 1998	Ole Gunnar Solskjaer	v. Newcastle United (h)
16 Sept. 1998	Nicky Butt	v. Barcelona (ECL) (h)
20 Sept. 1998	Nicky Butt	v. Arsenal (a)
12 Dec. 1998	Gary Neville	v. Tottenham Hotspur (a)
7 Mar. 1999	Paul Scholes	v. Chelsea (FAC) (h)
14 Apr. 1999	Roy Keane	v. Arsenal (FAC) (n)
5 May 1999	Denis Irwin	v. Liverpool (a)

(ECL) European Champions' League, (fr) friendly match, (WCC) World Club Championship.

INDEX OF PLAYERS

INDEX OF PLAYERS

INDEX OF PLAYERS